Come and See

Come and See

A Photojournalist's Journey into the World of Mother Teresa

Linda Schaefer

PRESS

A Division of the Diogenes Consortium

SANFORD · FLORIDA

Published by DC Press
2445 River Tree Circle
Sanford, FL 32771
http://www.focusonethics.com
407-688-1156

A portion of the proceeds of *Come and See* will be donated to the Missionaries of Charity.

This book was set in Adobe Goudy
Cover design and composition: Jonathan Pennell
Editor: Carolyn Lea
Proofing: Carol A. Hacker
Special editorial assistance: Susan Hayes

For orders other than individual consumers, DC Press grants discounts on purchases of 10 or more copies of single titles for bulk use, special markets, or premium use. For further details, contact:
Special Sales — DC Press
2445 River Tree Circle, Sanford, FL 32771
TEL: 866-602-1476.

Library of Congress Catalog Number: 2003103586
ISBN: 1-932021-08-6

First DC Press Edition
10   9   8   7   6   5   4   3   2   1
Printed in Thailand

All Photographs © Linda Schaefer
Photograph on p. xx taken for Linda Schaefer by Sally Martin

***Come and See** is dedicated to my late husband
Ron Campbell who helped me see what was
most important in life — our relationship to God.
Our marriage was brief, but our short life together was
a journey of dedication and love.*

*I also dedicate this work to my mother and father,
Liv and Frank, who opened my eyes to the world,
and gave me the greatest gift of life.
I honor them in their journeys until we meet again.*

Contents

Preface

Come and See is the story of a woman's search for peace — in mind and heart.

Linda Schaefer's wonderful photographs and recording of her meeting with Mother Teresa of Calcutta and accepting Mother Teresa's invitation to share her ministry to the poorest of the poor will surely help others in search of inner peace in mind and heart to discover these gifts in our serving the least among us.

— *Bishop William G. Curlin*
Diocese of Charlotte,
North Carolina

Foreword

I first met Linda Schaefer in 1986 when The King Center in Atlanta hired her to photograph the events of our annual Martin Luther King, Jr. holiday programs. I was pleased to see that her photos conveyed a sense that this photographer was committed to capturing the "soul" of the events she covered. She clearly cared about the legacy of my husband, Martin Luther King, Jr., and it was eloquently expressed in her photos over the five years that she shot for us.

Linda's deeply felt interest in spirituality and her commitment to revealing its healing power through her craft made her a superb choice to document the work of Mother Teresa of Calcutta and her Sisters of Charity and Mother Teresa personally granted her a level of access allowed few photographers. With extraordinary sensitivity, she has captured the quiet courage, compassion, and remarkable humility of Mother Teresa, the Sisters, and volunteers as they serve the destitute and dying, along with vivid scenes of daily life and struggle in Calcutta, the "City of Joy." Linda's moving memoir of her journey and her time with Mother Teresa complement these beautiful photos with great concern for the dignity and humanity of her subjects.

In *Come and See: A Photojournalist's Journey into the World of Mother Teresa*, Linda Schaefer has created an inspiring testament to the redemptive power of unconditional love and compassion. The work of Mother Teresa, her Sisters of Charity, and their wonderful volunteers from all over the world is lovingly documented and preserved in these pages for posterity. How gratifying that their work continues in the immortal spirit of Mother Teresa in 550 of the Sisters of Charity homes around the world. May her still-vibrant legacy of service to humanity inspire generations to come.

— **Coretta Scott King**
Atlanta, Georgia

Dusk in Calcutta appeared like a bluish hazy cast over the buildings left behind when the British left. I recognized an ethereal kind of beauty in the city, despite the obvious problems of a sprawling city.

Introduction

"COME AND SEE" were the words Mother Teresa said to me in one of the most intimate moments I had with her. I didn't realize then that she had given me the very words to describe the journey that led me to her. At the time she said, "come and see," I thought she had me confused with someone else. Come and See is a program the Missionaries of Charity offers to young women interested in dedicating their lives to God through Mother Teresa's Order. It gives them the opportunity to live and work alongside the Sisters for a trial period to see if they can meet the challenges of this demanding lifestyle.

I had been in Calcutta working as a volunteer with the Missionaries of Charity for a few weeks, when I decided to approach Mother Teresa for the second time to ask permission to photograph the facilities operated by her order. Earlier, when I posed the question to her, she said, "I don't need photographers. I need volunteers." She then suggested that I work at Shishu Bhawan, one of her orphanages. Now I was determined to ask her again. After all, I knew that *she* never took "no" for an answer.

After lunch I climbed the stairs of Motherhouse to meet with Mother Teresa. A Sister went into the private rooms where the administrative work is carried out and returned with the 85-year-old leader of one of the world's largest humanitarian organizations. She looked at me with piercing eyes and with a sweep of her hand invited me to sit down next to her on a concrete bench.

I asked her again if I could photograph the work for a possible book. She asked, "Why?" And then she pointed out, "There are already many books. People are making too much money on them." I promised her that this would not be that kind of book. She tilted her head as she responded to me. "No" was all she said as she looked at me again with those penetrating eyes. That "no" was like an arrow piercing my heart; I felt as if I was going to evaporate in front of her. For me it was like the Divine Mother rejecting her child. I immediately burst into tears.

The white stucco headquarters for the Missionaries of Charity is located on Lower Circular Road — one of the busiest, most congested streets in Calcutta. On this particular day, police officers blocked the traffic because of a political demonstration. The Sisters continued hanging clothes on the rooftop despite the activity below.

I had flown half way across the world in search of the woman who for me symbolized the embodiment of unconditional motherly love, and at that moment the little girl inside of me felt crushed by that word "*no*" because I needed her acceptance as a mother figure.

Mother Teresa's rejection created in me a similar feeling to the one I held about my own mother's inability to give me the kind of support for which I had always yearned. I knew that my mother loved me, but I craved her acceptance of the woman I had become. If I could have given my mother the words I wanted to hear, they would have been, "Yes, Linda, you are an artist. Go into the world with this gift of yours and make beautiful photographs that express who you are. Even if you aren't perfect, and the photographs aren't perfect, you are on your own path, and I respect the journey you have chosen."

I struggled through the insecure process of carving out a niche in my chosen field. Material success was not my goal — nor status and wealth. My quest as a photographer led me in many directions as I searched for meaning in my life through documentary projects (such as those shot in Bosnia, Croatia, the Brazilian Amazon, the lost children of Rio de Janeiro, and during the 1988 U.S. presidential campaign).

And now, sitting beside Mother Teresa, I took her rejection personally. Was what I had to offer not significant or helpful to her mission? I began to cry and Mother Teresa comforted me as I apologized for my outburst.

She consoled me as a river of tears fell on her sloping shoulders. She leaned her head close to mine and holding my hands gave me an assignment. "Write a proposal about what you want to do. I will pray about this tonight, and you come back tomorrow."

At that moment, I sensed her motherly love radiating through her hands and warming my heart. It was inconceivable to me that Mother Teresa would take so much time out of her day to console a wounded woman who had come to Calcutta to find a place in her heart and in her world. To be given permission to photograph the institution she had created would be the greatest gift I could imagine. When I looked at her through my tears, I saw only love. Her physical form seemed so inappropriate, almost like an illusion for those who couldn't see beyond the manifestation she presented to the world.

That afternoon I sat in the middle of the narrow bed in my hotel and tried to put into words the desire that was in my heart. I realized this was a frightening experience. Who was I to write about and photograph this living saint, a woman I could never hope to understand or do justice to through my work? I wasn't an enlightened soul who walked the same path as Mother Teresa. I was a regular person struggling along life's bumpy roads, working toward obtaining

Mother Teresa stayed close to her Sisters just moments before taking their final vows to the order she founded — the Missionaries of Charity.

greater personal wisdom. Only God knew the significance of Mother Teresa's mission, and I hoped to play a minor role on that journey with a camera as my instrument.

I knew without a doubt that Mother Teresa was at a much higher level of consciousness than most of us and that she expressed her love for humanity through her actions more than through words. When I was in her presence, and saw the love reflected in her eyes, it gave me the incentive to reach for that place of inner peace.

I felt this experience with Mother Teresa was a part of my journey. I was on a lifelong quest in search of a living holy mother. With this awareness of my mission, I was ultimately building my own spiritual strength as a woman. I had always admired Mother Teresa for her unconditional love for all humans and for the humbleness of her character. For me she represented the perfect earth mother — protector of all of her children.

Early the next morning I walked to Motherhouse with the few papers in hand, hoping to convince Mother Teresa that my motivations were pure and that my purpose was not to take advantage of her name or organization.

Once again, Mother Teresa joined me on the concrete bench outside her office. She glanced at the first page and then looked at me in the most hopeful manner. "Are you truly committed?" she asked. "Yes, yes," I responded, my heart pounding in anticipation of her decision. "It's very hard work," she continued and I nodded in agreement. "We have a program here called *Come and See*. You can come and try us out."

It then dawned on me that she was suggesting that I become a nun! "No, no, Mother Teresa, I'm a photographer. We talked yesterday." With a surprised look she responded, "Oh yes," as if only now recalling our conversation. She then went to the window of her office and asked a Sister for a piece of paper. It was an almost transparent pink sheet, upon which she wrote, "Dear Sisters, Please allow Linda Schaefer to photograph the work. God Bless You, Mother Teresa."

I knew at that moment that Mother Teresa was half joking with me, because the Order doesn't accept women my age into the *Come and See* program. Some people might have thought that her memory was faltering, but I knew that she was completely aware of what she was saying.

Later, I would realize that by suggesting that I "come and see," she was testing my sincerity and that she would require the same kind of commitment from me as she would from anyone involved with her organization. *Come and See* is the gift she offers to thousands of volunteers, visitors, and most importantly, prospective Sisters. It is the opportunity to be a part of an experience that is difficult to articulate or to even imagine from inside the safe walls of one's own reality.

Mother Teresa gave everyone who found the courage to "come and see" the chance to open their hearts through the direct experience of seeing the suffering as well as the joy inside of the walls of her homes for the dying, the neglected, the homeless, the sick, and the abandoned.

A smiling Mother Teresa with photographer Linda Schaefer.

Permission to photograph the
work of the Missionaries of Charity
in Mother Theresa's handwriting

CHAPTER 1

Photography — My Avenue to Love

ONE OF MY ASSIGNMENTS was to produce a video feature for Cable News Network on Indian spirituality. CNN had previously aired several news stories that I had written based on my experience with Catholic missionaries, who worked with the indigenous people in the Brazilian Amazon.

After working with people and organizations of different faiths, and after covering situations where people had been divided by their religious beliefs, I had come to terms that there are many paths to God, and there is no one right way.

By now, I felt prepared to finally meet the person whom I considered the greatest missionary of them all, Mother Teresa. I considered her to be free of religious prejudice, and for that reason she was a magnet for people of all faiths. As author Navin Chawla wrote in a biography of Mother Teresa: "We cannot view her through Catholic eyes, or Hindu eyes, but only through human eyes, for she does not discriminate. She respects all religions and all people …. By not making her religion exclusive, Mother Teresa's compassion encompassed persuasions and the irreligious and disbelievers as well."

I got my first break when Jay Suber, Vice President at CNN who was in charge of feature shows, gave me an assignment to cover five stories in India including a possible feature on Mother Teresa's work. I was grateful at the prospect of making some money on this trip, but I considered my trip to Calcutta as a pilgrimage more than as an opportunity to cover a story. Very often as a photographer, I had been assigned to photograph in soup kitchens or in shelters crowded with the homeless on the coldest nights. Perhaps this was in

In India, the streets alongside the temples are constantly bustling with activity. A small sign hanging on the wall of Kalighat — the home for the dying — indicates Mother Teresa's presence at one of India's busiest temples. A mother hugs her small boy outside the entrance of the home, while merchants work near the main door, and a beggar squats on the steps.

Seattle University student, Debbie Brown found that what she gave as a volunteer could never match what she received in return.

The main indication that a home for the dying exists inside the temple of Kali, is the crucifix on the roof of the temple with the hand-painted words, "I Thirst." When offered the empty rooms of the temple Mother Teresa gladly accepted what was a popular center of prayer for Hindus and started the Home for the Dying within twenty-four hours.

The Indian people are extremely open and friendly. I was completely at ease photographing their active lifestyles, as well as the quiet moments around community and companions.

preparation for the day I would *come and see* Mother Teresa's Mission in Calcutta. I would find that not all the photography assignments in the world could have completely prepared me for Calcutta and Mother Teresa.

As Linda Schaefer the photographer — not always as Linda Schaefer the woman — I see the goodness in people through my camera lens. When I'm focused on a person's eyes, it is like a suspended moment in time for me, as I see a glimpse of the essence of that person. According to Hindu tradition, the *atma* is the divine force within us all that connects us to God. God-realization or self-realization is dispelling the illusion that we are different and separate from each other and from God.

I realize that for me photography has been a gift, offering a divine perspective on the world. It has also helped me get beyond my own ego and to see people with greater compassion. My work has allowed me to enter people's lives that I would otherwise have never known.

My heart had to be opened, at least partly, before I would be ready for Mother Teresa. But when I found myself on the path, the obstacles seemed to become harder, and the tests more frequent. Mother Teresa showed me what I still lacked in my own character — forgiveness through love and giving without expectations of any returns.

For her it wasn't enough to say the words, *I love you.* It was her position that you've got to put them into action everyday. "We have to love until it hurts," she would say. We must put that love into a living action. And how do we do that? As Mother Teresa was often heard to say, "Give until it hurts."

Going to Calcutta would also bring up pain from my past. When I walked through the doors of Kalighat, Mother Teresa's home for the dying and destitute, I saw a room full of patients, many of them suffering and near death. It reminded me of my own husband's death to cancer, and with it the realization that I had never given myself permission to grieve. I didn't think that I could face that experience again.

Mother Teresa sent me to work as a volunteer at Kalighat for three months. Instead of it being a traumatic experience, it became a healing experience. By giving the patients the same kind of attention and love I had given my husband, I was able to overcome the dreaded feeling of imminent death. I saw that death could be a beautiful experience.

Mother Teresa provides shelters where people can die in peace with dignity. I began to view life and death as continuous cycles of each soul's journey. After the time at Kalighat, I found myself reviewing the process I had gone through with my husband, and now with less pain, it reminded me of why I first came to India.

Mother Teresa's original mission, called Nirmal Hriday ("the place of the pure heart") has treated over 100,000 people since 1950. Sisters pick the dying off the street and give them a home to die in peace and with dignity. "Heaven is found by serving the lowliest, the poorest of the poor."

A common sight in India — the destitute and dying lying on the streets. These are the men, women, and children the Missionaries of Charity find and transport to one of the many facilities. Known as the Saint of the Gutters, Mother Teresa said she saw the face of Jesus in everyone.

Mother Teresa in pew next to Sister Nirmala Joshi (who succeeded her as the new superior general of the Missionaries of Charity). When Mother Teresa visited Atlanta and spoke at Sacred Heart Church, she refused a seat near the altar, but elected to sit with her Sisters.

CHAPTER 2

Divine Coincidence —
Mother Teresa's Atlanta Trip

I N THE EARLY SUMMER OF 1995 I began to plan my fourth trip to India. And then, out of the blue, I received a phone call from Gretchen Keiser, editor of *The Georgia Bulletin*, the Archdiocese's newspaper for greater Atlanta. She said Mother Teresa was coming to Georgia in a matter of days and asked if I could photograph the event. I just about fell on the floor; I was so excited. I had worked for Gretchen over the past ten years as a photographer, and she knew how much I wanted to one day photograph Mother Teresa.

The night before her arrival in Atlanta I couldn't sleep. By 5:00 A.M. I was on my way to Hartsfield International Airport. At the last minute I had been given permission by her Order to photograph Mother Teresa at the airport. When the tiny corporate jet finally came into Atlanta's airspace, I ran out on the tarmac. The door opened, and there she was — dressed in the distinctive blue and white sari and wearing her frayed blue woolen sweater.

As a photographer, I'm accustomed to not drawing attention to myself as I work, so I was shocked when I saw Mother Teresa approaching me after shaking hands with Archbishop Donoghue and a number of priests. She held my hands with surprising strength. What I saw was the face of the *mother* and a look of unconditional love.

We drove in a police procession through the people-lined streets of Atlanta to her AIDS home in Virginia Highlands. Dozens of volunteers were already waiting for her; she greeted each one in the garden behind the home.

Later, during a Mass at Sacred Heart Church in downtown Atlanta, I sat by her feet with my cameras piled around my neck while she spoke from a podium in the sanctuary. I hardly heard what she said. I was too mesmerized by her presence. I gazed at her face, at her feet, and at her hands. She was real, she was here, and I was going to see her again in Calcutta.

* * * *

10

Ironically Mother Teresa flew into Atlanta on a corporate jet on loan from an executive. Dressed in one of her three cotton saris, "trademark" blue sweater and worn sandals, she was greeted as royalty.

Under cloudy skies, Mother Teresa was all smiles as she greeted Archbishop Donoghue of Atlanta. The colors of the Delta Air Lines umbrellas seemed more than coincidental.

Hundreds of the faithful gathered around Sacred Heart Church to catch a glimpse of Mother Teresa. A policeman pulls an Indian woman to her feet who attempted to kneel in an act of worship.

Archbishop Donoghue took Mother Teresa's hand and led her through the roped off crowds. The diminutive figure could barely be seen through the wave of journalists and supporters.

Mother Teresa often remarked that she was only a Sister — a pencil in God's hands. When she prayed during the Mass at Atlanta's Sacred Heart church, all eyes were turned toward her, but Mother Teresa, deep in prayer was oblivious to all the stares.

The Archbishop accepted a humble kiss on his hand from Mother Teresa — a person who never viewed herself as special.

Each volunteers at the AIDS hospice home in Atlanta was greeted by Mother Teresa. One lucky boy received a special blessing from her — an act he would carry in his heart forever.

This was my first moment alone with Mother Teresa — merely two hours after her at arrival in Atlanta. She was led to a room at the church to rest for a few moments before addressing the parish. I couldn't believe my good fortune to be alone in her presence, and snapped a photo in a photographer's moment.

As she addressed the audience at Sacred Heart, I sat near Mother Teresa, my eyes fixed on her feet. I couldn't take my gaze from her tiny feet, deformed by arthritis and squeezed into an old pair of leather sandals. She refused new sandals — instead having the old ones repaired over and over again.

A typical street scene in Calcutta, The city wakes to the sounds, smells, and color of a new day.

CHAPTER 3

Arrival in India

❋ ❋ ❋

WORDS OF MOTHER TERESA rang in my head as I prepared to fly to India. She had said that Western societies had the spiritually poorest of the poor. While they might not have the most physically poor, rich nations produced spiritually poor people. It was also her position that while one might offer food and shelter to the truly poor, it was a difficult task to take away the anger, bitterness, and loneliness those people feel.

On August 22, 1995, I was on a Lufthansa plane bound for India. Before I left Atlanta, the Sisters from the AIDS home gave me gifts to deliver to Mother Teresa. One of the gifts was a box of Godiva chocolates — one of her few indulgences.

During my ten-hour layover in the Frankfurt airport, I had a couple of petty arguments with women who worked in the terminal. The first was with a sales clerk who impatiently cleared the counter of face creams because I didn't make my selection quick enough. Another argument was with a Lufthansa employee who wouldn't let me sit in an area that was cordoned off, even though at the time there were no other seats available in the terminal. I reacted with hostility to these women when I perceived their individual aggressive behaviors.

When I boarded the plane for Bombay, within minutes of our departure, an Indian man dressed in blue jeans and a blazer left his seat and sat next to me. He looked at me and greeted me with a familiar look. Without hesitation he remarked, "You had a very bad week. It was very hot where you were." He was right. I had been trying to move and pack in temperatures that were over 100 degrees Fahrenheit in Georgia.

Never taking a pause he continued, "Your prayers saved your father. It could have been yes, or it could have been *no*." I was caught completely off guard and

unable to ask how he knew about these circumstances. My father had been recently hospitalized for heart failure and I nearly canceled my plans to return to India. I had cried and prayed to God to save his life.

He said that he was aware of my episodes with the women in Frankfurt and gave me some advice, "You must always be sweet, like me. You see they bring me chocolates." The airline attendants were hovering over him and giving him expensive candies. This brought to mind the Godiva chocolates I was bringing half way across the world to Mother Teresa.

Then came the real shock. This stranger told me I would soon have a baby and that it would fill the void in my heart. I told him that was impossible. Secretly I wanted a baby more than anything in the world. By this time in my life I had accepted the bitter fact that I would probably never have a child. But months later my second husband, and I would discover that I was indeed pregnant and I would be eventually returning to Atlanta with our son Paul in my womb.

India

After six weeks in a spiritual community in southern India, I was not close to my goal of traveling to Calcutta in search of Mother Teresa. I planned several detour trips with friends, but each time I was ready to depart, I became ill and couldn't travel.

It wasn't until a Danish woman, Vivian, confronted me with my fear of facing the monumental challenge of going to Calcutta that I finally made the arrangements to make the trip. She said, "Go and do what you're supposed to do. Write your book." She also told me to go before it was *too late*. In our last conversation, she

As the Missionaries of Charity grew, the need for a centralized building became a primary objective. A Muslim man sold his house inexpensively allowing the large white stucco building to become the headquarters for the Mission.

said that ultimately we all have to make the journey alone, and this was one I was meant to take by myself.

In my heart I knew Mother Teresa wasn't another photo opportunity, but a messenger from God who embodied the characteristics of the *Mother*. And now I was ready to make the journey, even if I was frightened beyond comprehension. I no longer seemed to be in total control of my destiny. I was ready to take the next step that would help lead me in the direction of surrender to God's will. It brought to mind something I had read about not attempting to control God's actions nor questioning the paths taken along the journey that he would take me. Even though one would desire to live a saintly life, it is God's choice if that ever occurs and the means taken to get to that point in life.

Touchdown in Calcutta

When my plane descended into the severely polluted air of Calcutta, I had no idea if Mother Teresa was even in the city. It was one of those rare moments where I was relying on pure faith. It was midnight, and I had made no advance reservations in Calcutta. I found a seedy guesthouse near the airport and slept fitfully through the night on a moldy mattress.

Early the next morning a taxi drove me through the chaotic streets of Calcutta in search of Mother Teresa's headquarters, affectionately known as Motherhouse — a term used to describe the central structure of every religious order or congregation. I was surprised to discover it was a gracious white stucco building overlooking one of Calcutta's busiest streets, Lower Circular Road. Several beggars insisted on carrying my camera bags to the front door. A Sister who answered the doorbell didn't seem at all surprised by my request for an audience with Mother Teresa.

She led me through a cool courtyard and up the stairs to the administrative offices. I was stunned. There stood Mother Teresa talking and laughing with an Indian family. She saw me out of the corner of her eye and signaled for me to wait on a nearby bench.

Drenched in perspiration at this early hour, I would have eagerly waited on that bench for an eternity — despite my normally impatient nature. Now here at last, almost within reach, I was overwhelmed by my great fortune to be so close to this living saint. To me this was confirmation that a higher power was guiding me along this path.

22

I n one of Mother Teresa's homes, a Sister quietly reads near her dormitory room. Sisters are encouraged to take time for contemplation, prayer, and rest during the day as a break from their grueling duties.

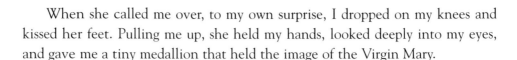

When she called me over, to my own surprise, I dropped on my knees and kissed her feet. Pulling me up, she held my hands, looked deeply into my eyes, and gave me a tiny medallion that held the image of the Virgin Mary.

I gave her the box of Godiva chocolates and then reminded her that I was the photographer from Atlanta, and that I hoped to document her work. She told me first to go to work in Shishu Bhawan, one of the Mission's orphanages. In my entire life I had never taken care of an infant, but of course I agreed.

A woman of few words, Mother Teresa turned and disappeared into her office. I was left alone and a slight panic set in as I considered my next steps. The Sister in charge of volunteers gave me names of inexpensive hotels where many of the volunteers stayed. She also said that within minutes a group of Sisters was leaving for the airport and that I could accompany them to pick up the remainder of my luggage at the guesthouse.

After two Sisters and I waved good-bye to the travelers, we got back into the ambulance that also served as transportation for the Missionaries of Charity. I didn't realize then that the Sisters rarely wasted an opportunity to check on one of the Mission's facilities.

One of the homes for severely retarded adults and children is located near the airport, so they decided to stop with some supplies. I was left to tour the facility alone. I pulled out my video camera — respectfully careful to avoid scenes that were too graphic. There were half-naked women napping on the ground, but when I entered the room they quickly got up and ran toward me, expecting the customary hug. I embraced several of them. This was clearly a rare and intimate view of how Mother Teresa and her followers worked. Women who could have been abandoned or neglected by family and society had been given a home.

I also saw babies and children sleeping contentedly in immaculate cribs. None were crying out of hunger or neglect. I watched as a woman — a lay volunteer who seemed to run the facility — showered attention and love on the curled up figures in the cribs. Each of the homes that I would visit or in which I would volunteer demonstrated that same kind of warmth, cleanliness, and sense of being a home — not an institution.

Back in the sunlight the Sisters suddenly appeared and told me it was time to leave. We parted at Motherhouse, and I went in search of the first of my many hotels in Calcutta — The Dolphine. For roughly five dollars (U.S.) per night, I was given a non-air-conditioned room. I tentatively unpacked one suitcase, showered, changed, and returned to the Motherhouse for the Hour of Adoration.

The prayer room was modestly arranged. A simple altar with a crucifix presided over the long, rectangular room. A beautiful statue of Mother Mary

24

This starving man had positioned himself outside the Kalighat temple near the home for the dying. He would be one of the fortunate ones to be given a sanctuary within the home.

faced the side of the room where the volunteers sat. Across from us the novices and Sisters knelt or sat cross-legged on the floor.

When I took my sandals off outside the door and walked into the room, I saw Mother Teresa alone on a straw mat near the door. She was bent over, deep in prayer, a rosary hanging from her curled up hand. She seemed oblivious to the stares of newcomers like me.

It was a mesmerizing hour. Although not Catholic, I held my own plastic rosary, and for the first time that day, felt completely at peace. That first night I walked back to my hotel knowing in my heart that destiny had brought me to the right place.

25

Beggars are found outside all temples throughout India with their metal pots waiting to be filled with food or coins. Location on the street is considered very important.

Everyday of the year masses of worshippers line up outside temples with offerings or *prasadam* for the gods and goddesses. Countless festivals draw even larger crowds that arrive wearing their finest clothes and jewelry. Throughout India each day begins and ends with prayer.

Early morning one finds worshippers descending the *ghats* or steps leading to the Ganges to bathe and conduct spiritual-centered activities. Several massage therapists have a thriving clientele near the bathers.

Relaxing on a street corner in a part of Calcutta known as the "City of Joy."

Becoming a *Sadhu* or holy man is considered a socially acceptable avocation for men and requires leaving the material world behind. Considered a worthy direction to take in life, the pious *sadhus* often live in the temples as monks or beggars.

28

The ancient city of Varanasi has been viewed as the Jerusalem or Mecca of India and millions make the annual pilgrimage to this holy place along the Ganges River. Many believe that all who die in Varanasi are given liberation or freedom from the cycle of birth and death.

As the sun rises each morning, the streets of Calcutta come alive with the most entrepreneurial of endeavors. The highly motivated street vendors display their wares — in this case selling eel.

The *sadhus* or holy men crowd the city ghats with their pots, begging for enough rupees to feed themselves.

On a morning walk through the "City of Joy," one can observe, amid the many vendors and open sewers, Muslim children attending classes in their school in the streets.

Taking a break from his chores at the leper colony at Titagarh, one of the residents gives a handsome smile for the camera.

This man's father has died and in preparation for the funeral on the banks of the Ganges, his head is shaved in Hindu tradition. He sits amidst the debris of flowers discarded on the ancient steps following an earlier ceremony.

A typical Calcutta street scene early in the morning. Fire hydrants are opened and buckets or metal pots are used to collect water to shower the bathers.

One of Mother Teresa's ardent followers commented, "We cannot view her through Catholic eyes or Hindu eyes, but only through human eyes, for she does not discriminate, she respects all religions and all people. By not making her religion exclusive, Mother Teresa's compassion encompassed persuasions and the irreligious and disbeliever's as well." Mother Teresa herself said, "I do convert. I convert you to be a better Hindu, a better Catholic, a better Muslim or Jain or Buddhist. I would like to help you find God. When you find Him, it is up to you to do what you want with Him."

In India, the elderly are revered as spiritual heads of the family.

For thousands of Indian men, life revolves around the temples and personal sacrifice in order to grow closer to God.

33

34

This is "Divine River" — the Ganges — provides space for commerce, bathing, disposal of the dead, and a reverent source for ritual prayer each morning and evening, despite the obvious physical conditions that might give westerners pause.

The face of Calcutta: to me, this boy is the embodiment of all the children of Calcutta to whom Mother Teresa extended her love and compassion.

CHAPTER 4

Shishu Bhawan

EARLY THE NEXT MORNING I hailed a rickshaw and was taken to the Motherhouse. I asked the man pulling the rickshaw to stop first at a coffeehouse along the way. I hadn't slept most of the night and knew that I would have to find a new hotel for the next night.

I was surprised to find that the streets were already alive and bustling with traffic. The cracked sidewalks were crowded with people bathing themselves around fire hydrants that had been opened for that purpose. This was also my first experience on a rickshaw, and I felt sad that this poor, bare-footed man, acting as a human horse, was pulling me through the streets of Calcutta.

After two cups of coffee we made our way onto Lower Circular Road and I was left at the main entrance of the Motherhouse. The morning began with 5:30 A.M. Mass followed by breakfast for the volunteers before they fanned out to the various facilities run by the Mission.

It was at breakfast over tea that I would meet my first fellow volunteers. I spoke with Kari Amber McAdam, a young student from Dartmouth College in New Hampshire who had received a fellowship to work with Mother Teresa. She was volunteering at Shishu Bhawan and offered to accompany me there after breakfast.

We walked the short distance to the orphanage and at that moment I felt frightened at the prospect of being around babies. I had never once changed a diaper. Kari on the other hand seemed like an old pro as I watched her handle a baby. The other volunteers also seemed very comfortable with the operation and their roles.

Several of Mother Teresa's orphans gather for a group photograph at Shishu Bhavan. One girl clutches a Western doll whose forehead has been painted with Hindu markings.

Orphans who have been in the orphanages for a brief period appear well fed and significantly healthier than when they first arrived. There are over forty houses for children throughout India as well as homes around the world for orphans.

Many of the children brought to the orphanages have been abandoned at hospitals, picked off the street, or from prisons. There are many special needs children, but none are turned away.

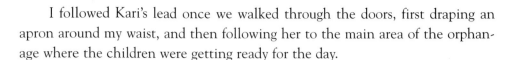

I followed Kari's lead once we walked through the doors, first draping an apron around my waist, and then following her to the main area of the orphanage where the children were getting ready for the day.

I was completely out of my league. Volunteers and nuns were pulling dozens of children out of their cribs. The Australian woman in charge was already delegating various duties to the volunteers. First, diapers had to be changed. Then the plastic mattresses had to be washed down. Large pots of porridge were already being ladled out as volunteers gathered up two or three children at a time to be fed.

I tentatively found a baby who thankfully didn't need much assistance, and began to feed her porridge with a spoon. "This can't be happening," I thought. But I plunged ahead, and found another child to feed. It suddenly occurred to me that if the Indian man's prediction was true, then this was a great training ground for that day when I'd have my own child.

But in that first hour, I didn't know if motherhood was really for me. It was exhausting work. After the children were fed, the Australian woman gathered them up and lined them up on wooden potties. They looked so cute and healthy, a far cry from the starving, malnourished children of the slums.

For the next two hours we played games with the children. There were very few toys, but human companionship, touching, and love were what they seemed to want most. I found myself on a verandah with some of the other volunteers, simply holding and cuddling the children, until it was time for lunch. After the children were fed and put to bed for their naps, we were allowed to leave. We would return when the children awoke.

Most afternoons I spent touring Calcutta or interviewing other volunteers about their experience with Mother Teresa. Most of them agreed that they were in Calcutta to see how Mother Teresa worked and hoped to walk away from this experience with a new sense of themselves and others. I even met one volunteer who was hoping to go through Mother Teresa's process of *come and see* so that she could become a Sister.

Kari Amber was one of the first volunteers I interviewed. She told me that she had always worked with children and hoped to make a difference in the lives of Mother Teresa's orphans. "However meager the difference I am making in their lives, there is a difference. Whether they recognize me two months from now or ten years from now doesn't really matter," she said. "To make them feel joy in a tragic setting (being in an orphanage) made the whole trip worthwhile for me."

At the other end of the spectrum of volunteers was Mary Ellen Moore, a woman in her sixties who lived in her own rented apartment in Calcutta while working as a volunteer. I met Mary Ellen at Shishu Bhawan where she assisted

At nineteen, Kari Amber McAdam, a Dartmouth College student, had no problem caring for several hungry children at once. Today, Kari is married and completing her doctorate in psychology.

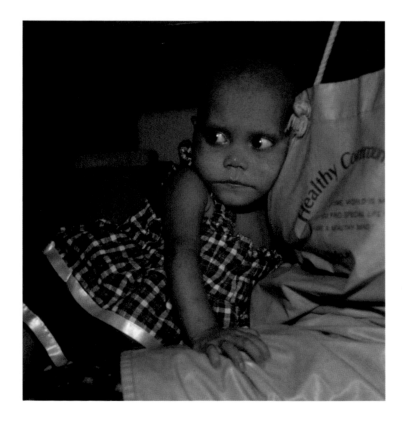

There are few toys at the orphanages, but an abundance of love and attention from the Sisters and volunteers.

the Sisters with administrative work. She responded in writing to the thousands of requests for adoptions from couples around the world.

I discovered from Mary Ellen that Mother Teresa had strict rules about whom she would adopt a child to and that included their nationality. For instance, Mary Ellen told me that as a rule Mother Teresa would not send her babies to American couples because of the high divorce rate in the United States. This struck me as an unfair rule. Later, through my experience with Mother Teresa, I realized her compassion extended to all people and countries. She was, however, often criticized for her views on such issues as contraception and abortion, as well as adoption. But her views didn't interfere with the work she was doing around the world. She wanted the best possible and most stable situations for her children.

I found my own views and opinions shifting as I worked as a volunteer. My sense of compassion for the children grew as I became more familiar with their faces. I was particularly drawn to a blind girl who seemed to recognize me each time I picked her up from her crib.

"In the United States people talk about compassion, but they only talk about it," said Mary Ellen during one of our numerous conversations. "They don't put it into action because of their fear. Sometimes people don't even realize they're afraid." She said that fear prevents people from extending themselves in a crisis, and until they can admit to this emotion and break through the fear, they are incapable of giving compassion or love.

A nurse by profession with a background in hospice work, Mary Ellen also helped the Sisters in Kalighat — the home for the dying. An apron over her stylish outfit, I saw Mary Ellen bandaging wounds on the frail arms and feet of the women.

"There is a difference between pain and suffering," she told me. "The people at Kalighat showed me pain without suffering because they don't have any expectations." She also shared her experiences at Kalighat with hospice workers in the United States. "You can't help them unless you get inside of them." Later, I would also serve as one of the volunteers at Kalighat and would see firsthand how tremendous pain could be alleviated by boundless love and attention.

And that is exactly how Mother Teresa helps her volunteers, by giving them the opportunity to learn compassion without judgment, fear, or pity. "As soon as you pity someone, you put yourself above that person," Mary Ellen observed during another of our conversations.

I moved into the Fairlawn Hotel for a two-week respite from the heat and overwhelming fatigue that I was experiencing. I met Sally Martin — another volunteer in her sixties — at the Fairlawn, a quaint and charming bed and

41

Sishu Bhavan, the Home for the babies, grew from the first facility to over forty houses throughout India — as well as the rest of the world. The unwanted children are found on the streets or brought to the homes where they are provided love and attention they would not have found outside. Many have gone on to various occupations, receive advanced educations, and become loving parents.

The healing power of touch: Dana Jarvis, an elementary school teacher from Chicago gives special needs children the attention they so desperately need and wouldn't get on the streets.

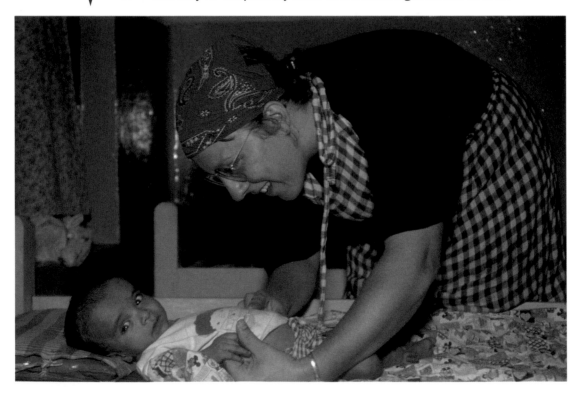

breakfast-style facility run by a British couple who had made Calcutta their home prior to India's independence in 1949.

I frequently met Sally over lunch and her humorous manner and laissez-faire attitude helped me overcome some of my much too serious perspective at that moment. Sally was taking a two-week break from her year-long bicycle tour around the world to volunteer at Mother Teresa's orphanage. "I had another month to bike around Greece. I read three guidebooks on India, and this one said that if you just went and knocked on the door of Mother Teresa's residence, that they would let you in and put you to work. That sounded really good. It would be so different from bike touring. I feel that when I'm bike touring, I'm doing it for myself. It's a completely selfish thing to do. Going to work for Mother Teresa would be just the opposite," she said.

After breakfast Sally and I would walk to Shishu Bhawan and as the days passed I would find myself laughing more. Sally's contagious easy going manner also affected the children. She played Simple Simon with them, and soon they would all be laughing and waving their arms in the air.

Sally was also more than willing to be my companion over the next two weeks when when I was touring Calcutta. We visited the *ghats*, the famous bathing steps along the Ganges River, and even attended a funeral ceremony at one of the crematorium *ghats*.

We also visited an area of Calcutta, near the Howrah railroad station, made famous in the book *City of Joy*. Sally carried one camera bag, while I photographed familiar street scenes depicted in the book, including the open sewers and the children who followed us along the alleyways. At the end of one street we saw the familiar sign indicating that the Missionaries of Charity housed an orphanage there.

We entered the orphanage, walked upstairs, and found a group of volunteers playing with the children. We found women from Spain, Denmark, Ireland, and the United States. Fernanda, a medical doctor from Spain, told me that she was here as a volunteer not a doctor. "I see that so many people need help, so I felt that I had to do something."

Some of the women had already volunteered for Mother Teresa and were here for a second tour of duty, and looking forward to a third. I met a seventy-nine-year-old woman from Australia who had been working with Mother Teresa's orphans for many years — but insisted that this was the last time!

I only encountered one man working as a volunteer at Shishu Bhawan. I met Jean Danielle at the Salvation Army hostel, where many of the volunteers lived on a shoestring budget — staying for about one dollar (U.S.) per night. Jean told me that because of his background as a physical therapist, he could help some of

43

"**L**ove until it hurts…. What I do you cannot do; but what you do, I cannot do. The needs are great, and none of us, including me, ever do great things. But we can all do small things, with great love, and together we can do something wonderful."

— **Mother Teresa**

A nurse shares a special moment with a two tiny residents at Shishu Bhavan. Touch is one thing that cannot be given too often to these children.

44

Inga, a Danish student studying to become a social worker, remarked, "I was here four years ago and wanted to come back. Most of the time I work at the home for the dying. It gives my life meaning to help people."

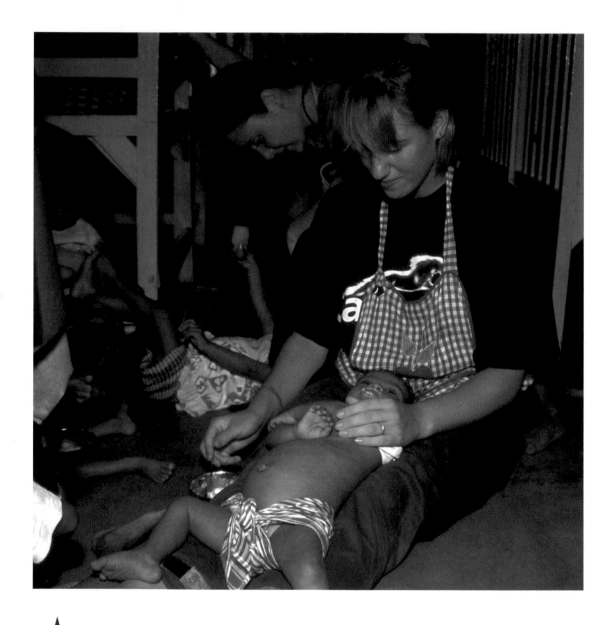

46

There are very few toys at the orphanages, but plenty of love and personal attention. The cloth diapers are made by the lepers at the Missionaries of Charity colony outside Calcutta.

the handicapped children. He was planning to spend about three months working for Mother Teresa.

"In our own world we would never come together. But we come here and work and live together, and become friends." Jean found that politics, race, and religion never interfered in the volunteers' ability to work together. Jean believed that Mother Teresa loved all people regardless of their nationality or faith and that is what attracted the wide range of people who worked for her as volunteers.

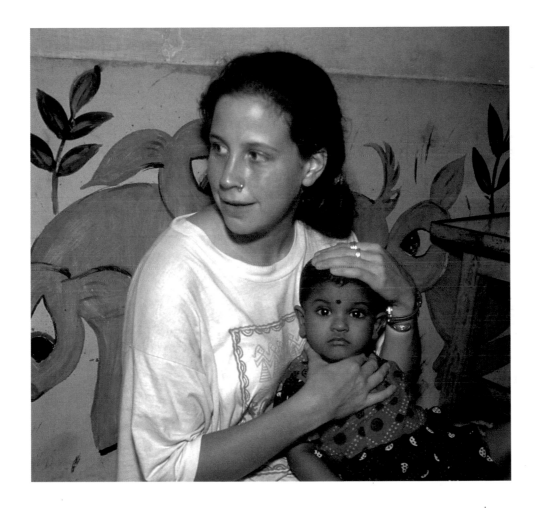

Tara, an American nurse, recently graduated from James Madison University in Virginia, told me "I heard a lot about volunteering for Mother Teresa from other travelers. I'm Catholic and I was interested to see how Catholicism works in India. It's much more traditional here. I plan to work with children in the future."

47

Mother Teresa in deep contemplation moments before the Mass during which the novices would take their final vows and become Sisters.

CHAPTER 5

Missionaries of Charity

✳ ✳ ✳

T HE LONGER I STAYED WITH MOTHER TERESA, the more I wanted to learn about her organization, how it was founded, and Mother Teresa the woman. It is well known that Mother Teresa doesn't like to talk about herself, but I found a beautiful authorized biography about her, written by an Indian Hindu, Navin Chawla, who received permission to write a book about her life and work. He gives an in-depth insight into Mother Teresa's boundless determination to help those most in need and how she went about organizing a multitude of centers in Calcutta and around the world.

They include homes for abandoned children; homes for the dying and destitute; medical dispensaries for lepers and tuberculosis patients; a colony for lepers run by Brothers of the Missionaries of Charity; and a prison for female inmates (which Mother Teresa was able to convince the Communist government of Calcutta to turn over to her control).

When the Missionaries of Charity's Constitution was approved by the Sacred Congregation in Rome, it included a fourth vow — wholehearted and free service to the poor. Mother Teresa's order began on October 7, 1950. Over the decades, close to 500 centers were established in more than 100 countries.

Shishu Bhawan is the name for the many children's homes throughout India. The Mission works closely with adoption agencies overseas and even handicapped children are usually placed. In the early days Mother Teresa herself would accompany the children overseas to meet their new families. Very often babies are brought to the Sisters on the verge of death, which brings the following quote from Mother Teresa to mind: "For me even if a child dies within minutes, that child must not be allowed to die alone."

✳ ✳ ✳ ✳

Mother Teresa — Born to be a Nun

Mary Teresa Bojaxhiu was born August 26, 1910 in Skopje, Yugoslavia when it was a part of the kingdom of Albania. As a child she was known as Gonxha — "flower bud" — and at the age of twelve first felt the desire to become a nun. She heard of the Loreto nuns who worked as teachers in India. At eighteen she left home forever to pursue a life dedicated to God. Before she could go to India and serve, she first entered the Loreto Abbey in Rathfarman, Ireland in 1928.

A group of novices sing at the Motherhouse. All participate in several hours of prayer and contemplation each day.

Eventually her prayers were answered and she became a Loreto Sister in Calcutta. After twenty years she felt a deeper calling — to work with the poorest of the poor. That was on September 10, 1946. "It was an inner command to renounce Loreto where I was very happy, to go serve the poor in the streets. The message was clear. It was an order. I was to leave the convent. I felt God wanted something more from me. He wanted me to be poor and to love Him in the distressing disguise of the poorest of the poor."

Near the end of July 1948 she received permission from the Vatican to leave the safe walls of the Loreto Convent and she headed straight for Motijhil, a slum on the outskirts of Calcutta. It was there that she set up her first classroom and drew the letters of the alphabet in the sand with a stick.

It was not long before she saw that other needs of the poor required immediate attention. Soon there was a dispensary for the sick, particularly to servely ill tuberculosis patients and lepers that were given no other medical attention. In time other women were drawn to Mother Teresa, and with their help she quickly started organizing what would soon become one of the largest organizations in the world: the Missionaries of Charity.

Familiar as any faces seen on the streets of Calcutta, sisters return to the Motherhouse after attending Mass at St. Mary's.

As young women might do anywhere in the world, novices enjoy a moment together to chat outside the home for the dying in Calcutta.

* * * *

52

A group of Sisters supervise the unloading of sacks of grain (a gift of the United States) from one of their ambulance/buses on Lower Circular Road.

The Missionaries of Charity and Mother Teresa

On October 7, 1950 the Constitutions for the Missionaries of Charity were approved by Rome and three years later the new Order moved into permanent headquarters on Lower Circular Road.

Mother Teresa has always refused any effort of fundraising, and the Superior of each region where the Missionaries of Charity have homes distributes all donations. "I don't want the work to become a business. It must remain a work of love," she said. Mother Teresa also never accepted funding from the government or the Church. Both would have involved keeping accounts and distracting the Sisters from their work.

In Calcutta alone, there are nine houses. A Superior runs each house, and a number of houses are placed under a Regional Superior. Each Regional Superior is in charge of a Province, e.g., Western Europe, America, and Africa. As Mother Teresa put it, "God's work has to be done properly. If people can do it for money, why can't we do it for the love of God?"

Mother Teresa tried to step down twice as head of the organization, once in 1973, and then again in 1979 when her coronary problems began, but both times was persuaded to continue in her leadership role. When I met her in 1995, she was still traveling around the world visiting her houses. In less than two years she would step down from her position, and finally be given the rest she had needed for so long.

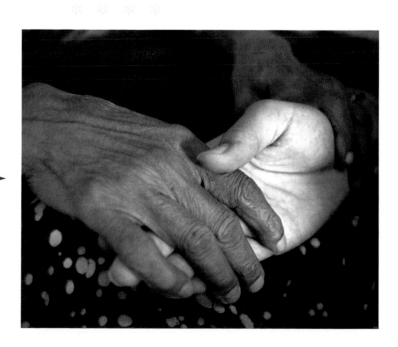

A volunteer holds the hand of a patient at the home for the dying. Mother Teresa said: "We can not do great things. We can only do little things with great love."

Love and joy can be found in every corner of Kalighat — the home for the dying — as a novice cares for a patient.

The soothing touch of another human is often one of the last acts of love shared between a patient and a Sister. A person's dignity means so much and everything is done to see that it is preserved at the house of the dying.

“India needs technicians, skilled men, economists, doctors, nurses, for her development. Meanwhile, the people have to live, they have to be given food to eat, to be taken care of, and dressed. Our field of action is the present India. While these needs continue, our work will continue.”

— **Mother Teresa**

Always discreetly present, Mother Teresa joins in a liturgical reading.

Mother Teresa, joined by Sister Nirmala (*far right*) who took over the leadership role of the Missionaries of Charities, blessed Sisters and the congregation at the end of a Mass.

Volunteers join the Sisters for Mass at the home for
the dying. On the chalkboard, next to a photo of
John Paul II and Mother Teresa, is written: "Every
act of love brings a person face to face with God."

E ach Sunday Mass is held at the home for the dying. Volunteers join the circle of local musicians for devotional singing before the Mass begins.

Mass at St. Mary's, Calcutta.

Train Ride to Titagarh — Gandhijhi Prem Nivas (Leper Colony)

NAVIN CHAWLA QUOTED MOTHER TERESA when she said, "Leprosy is not a punishment. It can be a very beautiful gift of God if we make good use of it."

Thursdays are the one official day of rest for the Missionaries of Charity and for the volunteers. It is also the day when many volunteers take the hour-long train ride to Titagarh to visit one of Mother Teresa's leper colonies, Ghandhiji Prem Nivas (Abode of Love).

During my stay in Calcutta, I visited the colony twice and had the opportunity to photograph and videotape interviews with patients, Brothers of the Missionaries of Charity, and numerous volunteers. It was a powerful journey for all of us who made it because we could truly see the extent of Mother Teresa's commitment to helping those most in need.

When she turned her attention to the plight of lepers in India, she was able to reverse an extremely sad predicament for some of the country's most neglected people into a positive and thriving enterprise. There are about 12,000,000 leprosy cases worldwide, most of them in Asia, with some 4,000,000 in India.

Mother Teresa set up her first mobile leprosy clinic in 1957, followed by the construction of facilities that would provide medical care, dormitories, schools for the children of lepers, and the resources that would make the lepers self-sufficient. Today there is a Missionaries of Charity leprosy station in most Third World countries.

The British built an enormous railroad network throughout India that still serves as the main form of long distance travel. It is also a magnet that attracts, among others, lepers who are often found by volunteers or the Brothers of the Missionaries of Charity, who either treat them medically or bring them to one of the leper villages.

Life for the lepers at villages such as Titagarh is good. In a society in which families and society abandons them — the disease viewed as a punishment — victims have found new lives within the haven of the communities.

At first glance, it is not obvious that most of the inhabitants of the village are lepers. They have been given a new lease on life. Volunteer doctors and the staff treat the disease and Sisters are given the tools to provide relief from the isolation leprosy creates.

The first time I accompanied a group of volunteers to Titagarh, it was also my first train ride in India. I felt as if I had to tune into another vibration level in order to adjust to the experience — the masses of people, the smells, the heightened sense of sounds and activity. I have found over the years that Indians are very tolerant people who easily adjust to most conditions. They don't seem to have the need for personal boundaries and privacy that Westerners crave. In this case I was at least hoping for a vacant seat to view the landscape. No such luck. Most of us stood, bouncing from side to side for the duration of the ride.

I had never met many of these volunteers. Some of them worked at Kalighat or at one of the other facilities. I was particularly interested in interviewing Debbie Brown, a student from Seattle University, who appeared to have a certain maturity about her for such a young woman.

During a train stop I had a chance to speak with her about her experience with Mother Teresa and the motivation that brought her here. "I was looking for something different than the lifestyle I was taught in America — there is so much wealth and so much waste. Even before coming here, it was difficult for me to live that way."

Debbie spoke modestly of her work as a volunteer at Kalighat. "My contribution with Mother Teresa is so small, but with so many people helping, we can together make a difference. But I also know that I will take so much more from this place than I can ever give."

When we finally arrived at our destination, it was a relief to get off the overcrowded train. It also felt like a much-needed break from the routine in Calcutta. Directly across the railway tracks I saw a beautifully painted arch with the words *Ghandhiji Prem Nivas*.

My creative instinct was immediately attracted by what I saw, and I pulled out my photography equipment as I began to feel the joy of doing my work in a place where Mother Teresa's presence was so strong. My group disappeared as I became absorbed with taking photographs.

I entered a huge, rectangular room, buzzing with activity. A dozen men, dressed only in *dhotis*, the traditional Indian male labor attire — yards of checkered cloth wrapped around their sweaty waists — were hard at work on ancient-looking looms. They were weaving the saris for the Missionaries of Charity Sisters worldwide. Across from them sat the women, deeply concentrated on their work as they spun miles of thread on the *charkhas* (the traditional Hindi spinning wheel that became a symbol of India's freedom when Mahatma Gandhi [Mohandas Ghandhiji] used it as a weapon of independence).

I videotaped close-ups of the men's hands as they skillfully wound pieces of thread through their fingerless hands. It was hard to believe that these men and women were actually lepers. It took several intensely focused moments for me to

65

66

This colorful oasis and fish pond provides a peaceful atmosphere for residents and workers at the Gandhiji Prem Nivas Leprosy Center established by Mother Teresa in 1958.

understand the reality of this situation. I gazed at a woman dressed in a colorful sari, a peaceful smile on her lips. And then I saw the wooden prosthetic leg leaning against the wall. It dawned on me that these people were in fact all lepers.

It was not the Biblical or even more recent image of a leper community. Mother Teresa had taken these once abandoned sick people off the streets, and off the railway tracks where they slept, and had given them back their lives.

It was in this room that I met George Van den Berg. He had arrived on an earlier train and had already toured the facility, but offered to accompany me through the other buildings. What I saw was not an institution, but a home, an oasis for hundreds of men and women who had once suffered from the stigma of their disease. With George I also found a very sympathetic and sincere companion by my side. I would learn much more about George in the weeks to come. He had saved his wages as a laborer in a potato factory in Holland to work for one year as a volunteer for Mother Teresa.

"This is a lesson for life," George told me as we walked between rows of banana trees. "Mother Teresa is an example for everyone; that's what attracted me to her. She does what she says. I want to try to live the way she lives. As she says, 'I must become less and less. Jesus must become more and more.' I thought that when I left Holland and knew that I was going to Calcutta, that I was someone special. But you come here and see there are so many volunteers. It changes your mind, and you realize that you're not so special. We have to be able to say, 'I'm not important and it's Jesus who is working through me.' Then you look at this service from a different point of view."

George and I entered the dormitory for men who were in need of medical attention. The room was immaculate, each bed neatly covered with one of the checkered cloths made by the lepers. We found a father and son who were both infected by the disease. They joined us outside overlooking a peaceful courtyard. The son said that he had been infected with the disease shortly after his wife gave birth to their daughter. That was ten years ago, and now his family lives with him at the colony.

There were few patients in the dormitory. Most were busy working at their particular trade within the compound. We saw men and women in the fields planting new crops. Not far from them there were women washing clothes in a pond. We also found a room where men were hand-cutting and stitching sandals.

As we continued our tour of the grounds, we walked past a building where we could hear the voices of children laughing. When we peered into the classroom we saw a boisterous group facing their patient teacher. He allowed me to videotape this very normal classroom scene. The only difference was that they were the children of lepers.

67

Mother Teresa created villages so that the lepers could live and work in peace — away from the scorn and rejection of society.

In spite of all the activity there was a sense of peace, as I had already found so noticeable in all the facilities run by the Missionaries of Charity. As I walked along the pathways with George, I heard birds singing, only to be interrupted for a moment by the sound of a train passing nearby. The air was filled with the sweet fragrance of jasmine. A statue of Gandhi (Ghandhiji) overlooked the pond with bright red hibiscus flowers adorning his marble face.

We ran into our group resting in a shaded garden. They were having a conversation with one of the Brothers of the Missionaries of Charity. He told me that eight Brothers ran this particular facility, with the responsibility for treating 200 live-in patients, and altogether there were 400 workers. The Brothers also give guidance to 30,000 outdoor cases. They are trained in pharmaceutical medicine and treat the patients themselves. However, when surgery is required, volunteer doctors bring their services to the colony.

We also spoke briefly to Brother Vinod who overseas the work at Ghandhiji Prem Nivas. He told me that he used to work in a bank and on the weekends began helping the Sisters of the Missionaries of Charity. "In the 1970s my desire to become a Brother began." He resigned his job at the bank and applied to work with Mother Teresa. That was twenty years ago. "This is much more worthy work," he said. "Look how many more I can serve now."

It was over thirty years ago, after visiting Titagarh, that Mother Teresa was convinced that she needed to do something to help the lepers. The Missionaries of Charity started with a small clinic near the railway lines. Then the Brothers of her Order took over the work with the lepers. They supervised the construction of buildings and developed the resources that would eventually give the patients an environment in which to live and work. Mother Teresa always wanted the families affected by leprosy to be self-sufficient and to have the means to keep themselves independent.

Titagarh, once a useless piece of land near the railway tracks, is today a thriving enterprise, where lepers live and work toward self-sufficiency and raise their own food.

On the train ride back to Calcutta, I couldn't help but reflect on this powerful experience. Each day I was being exposed to Mother Teresa's work, and I was amazed by her accomplishments. It occurred to me that while Mother Teresa was a world-

Seattle University student volunteer Debbie Brown sits Indian style on the train platform awaiting the train to the leper colony.

renowned figure, the fact remained that so few people truly understand the extent of her work. Even those of us that had come to see would only be exposed to a portion of the miracles she was creating in every corner of the world. The miracles were practical and compassionate solutions for those people who had no where else to turn.

As Mother Teresa said, "... we can learn to love the unloved, the unwanted; not only just to give them things but to make them feel that they, too, are useful, that they, too, can do something because they feel they are loved and wanted, that they can share the joy of loving."

A long, rectangular room houses dozens of the aging spinning wheels or *charkhas* — recognized as a symbol of India's freedom. Women sit cross-legged, spinning yarn that will eventually become the fabric of the Sister's saris.

Men, dressed in *dhotis,* the traditional male dress, work swiftly with deformed hands that have grown accustomed to working on the looms despite their impairment.

72

73

Patients at the leper colony take a mid-day rest before resuming their activities of making saris, clothing for the Sisters, diapers for children at the orphanages, and clothing worn by patients of the Missionaries of Charity worldwide.

It seemed almost impossible to see that this man had been afflicted with the dreaded disease leprosy. I found all the patients very willing to discuss their illness and the haven that Mother Teresa had provided for them.

The Town of Peace, which Mother Teresa established for rehabilitating lepers, covers thirty-five acres of land. Indian women (*above*) are often the construction workers, piling bricks on their heads and passing them in a circle.

The power of prayer. As a sign of welcome, Indians often place their palms together with the word *Namaste* — which translates as acknowledging the divine within. Despite their suffering, the lepers were very receptive to visitors.

"Suffering, if it is accepted together, borne together, is joy."

— **Mother Teresa**

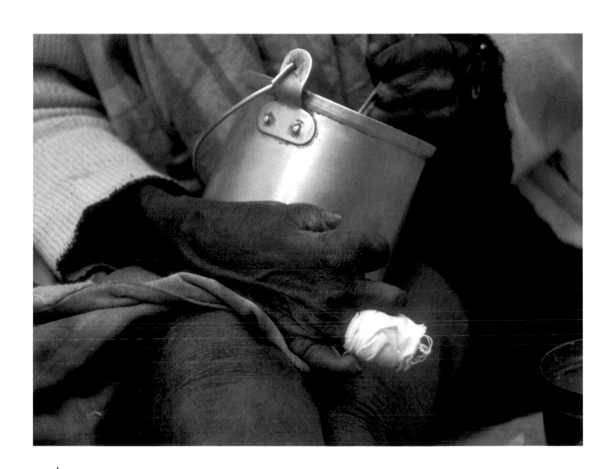

"**T**he work for the leprosy patients at the Titagarh Leprosy Home, was from the very start one of our main works."

— **Mother Teresa**

78

Lined up along Sudder Street — home to most of the volunteers — rickshaws wait for business. The world's oldest form of wheeled transportation, the Indian rickshaw remains the primary method of moving people from one place to another.

CHAPTER 7

Sudder Street

A FEW DAYS AFTER MY FIRST VISIT to Mother Teresa's leper colony, I began to visit some of the hotels and dormitories where many of the volunteers stay while in Calcutta. Sudder Street is the main tourist artery of Calcutta, particularly for young people traveling around India. There are what appear to be an endless number of cheap hotels and inexpensive restaurants that serve Western food. Sudder Street was my home for a few weeks while I stayed at the Fairlawn Hotel.

Directly across the street from my pleasant accommodations was the Salvation Army hostel, home for many young men who were working as long-term volunteers. One evening shortly after my first encounter with George, I visited him in his dormitory for the purpose of videotaping an in-depth interview with him. When I stepped through the front door, I immediately smelled the stale air and noted that the dusty walls were badly in need of painting. A guard pointed me in the direction of George's room that was on the ground floor facing noisy Sudder Street. George was lying on a narrow cot talking with several Frenchmen who also worked as volunteers with Mother Teresa.

Lines of rope hung from the walls, clothes piled over them, some drying, but most of the blue jeans had no other place to be stored except in suitcases that were under the beds or next to the cots. An old fluorescent light dimly lit the room, and a few tables were littered with plastic water bottles, shaving supplies, and bottles of shampoo.

The men seemed perfectly content in their surroundings as they lounged on their beds sharing their experiences as volunteers among themselves and then with me. I sat at the end of George's bed, flipped on my video camera, and let the men talk for the next hour. Their testimonies were profound and filled with their burning desire to find greater meaning in their lives.

Lying on his bed, an arm supporting his head, George began by telling me about an experience he had that morning with a patient at Kalighat. "He [the

80

Volunteer Kari Amber McAdam stayed at the Modern Lodge during the three months she served Mother Teresa. For a few dollars per day, it is one of the more inexpensive hotels on Sudder Street.

patient] took my hand and kissed it. I understood he knew he was going to die. I held his hand while he cried." At that moment George knew that the work with Mother Teresa was far more meaningful than the simple act of washing and feeding the patients.

In his own country George found his work at the potato factory unsatisfactory. "For me it's wonderful to do this work and to express the love I have inside." He believed that priests in Holland made too much money and that it interfered with their work. "If you want to be true to your religion, why not work for less? Mother Teresa does not ask for money. She says God is her banker. She gives all the donations to the poor and takes nothing for herself."

In regard to his work at Kalighat, George found that the environment did not depress him, but that it gave him greater peace of mind. "I would say to anybody — don't hesitate to come here because you are not only giving but you get a lot back."

The three Frenchmen joined in the conversation. The two brothers, Sam and Sebastian, were traveling with Jean Danielle and, besides working for Mother Teresa, were also affiliated with a French charitable organization that was in the process of setting up schools in the slums of Calcutta.

In addition to working at Shishu Bhawan, Jean Danielle was also volunteering at Prem Dum, a home for mentally handicapped men and women. "I feel that we have to live with the people we want to help," he said. "You don't have to be a doctor or a physical therapist to help. Everyone has something to give."

Sam, also a physical therapist and taking time out from his job at a hospital in France, was planning to stay in Calcutta for several months working as a volunteer. "No one wants to die alone. Mother Teresa gives them love, so that their pain is less when they don't have medicine."

Sebastian said the work was not tiring, but motivated him to want to do more. "There is no problem with differences of religion, racism, or nationality among the volunteers. We should get along like this in our own countries."

Jean Danielle added, "We all come from different social backgrounds, but here we come for the same thing — to work for Mother Teresa — and we work and live together. It's a great thing."

Sam said that he enjoyed the work. "It's fun doing charity work. In Europe people have no fun in their lives. Here we work together and feel that we're doing something good in our lives."

For the next half hour George had us mesmerized by his thoughts on Mother Teresa, Jesus, and the true purpose of religion and faith. I even asked him if he

Helping each other over the cracks and puddles that populate the streets of Calcutta.

Sisters returning home to the Motherhouse from Mass at St. Mary's Catholic Church.

had ever considered becoming a Brother. "It's not easy to be an instrument of God. We are more inclined to satisfy our egos — look at what I am doing. It's the other way around. We have to say, 'I'm not important, and it's Jesus who works through me.' Jesus said, 'If you do to the least of my brothers you do it to me.' Jesus is in the dying man or woman and in the orphan and in the lonely woman. And if you accept that, or confirm that within yourself, then you love from a different point of view."

All the men agreed that they had changed since coming to work for Mother Teresa. They felt that the positive energy and loving environments had stimulated them to become more loving themselves.

"They say when you go into the army you get the best out of yourself. Forget it — it is here where you get the best out of yourself," George laughed. "Mother Teresa has written on a piece of paper she hands out: *Give them their daily bread through our hands*. In my country, I learned — give us our daily bread."

We all agreed that there wasn't enough encouragement for that kind of action in our own countries, but that Mother Teresa encouraged everyone to help their fellow humans, regardless of their faith. "It's all about me doing something for somebody, and not asking God to do it," said George. "God needs us to do the work for him. He wants us to take action."

There are quotes by Mother Teresa and Jesus taped to the wall of all the facilities in Calcutta. One of them reads: *To feel the touch of God, we only need to touch each other*. "To Mother Teresa, it is her holy duty to relieve people all over the world," was George's final comment.

The Salvation Army is a home for an army of volunteers, men and women, who I found enriching their lives with each other, with Mother Teresa, and with their work.

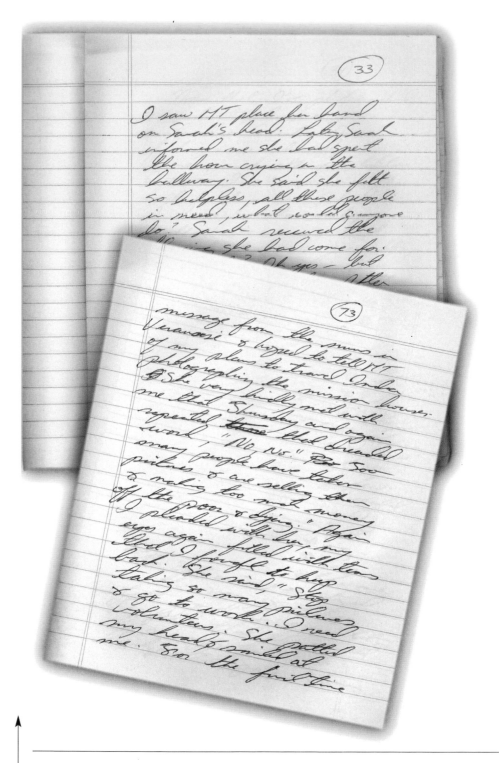

84

The daily journal kept by Linda Schaefer during her stay with Mother Teresa gives insight into events that most people never see. Page 33 of the journal tells of a volunteer, Sarah Torsin of Belgium, who felt overwhelmed by the death and dying around her and how the mere touch of Mother Teresa's hand on her head had a calming effect. Page 73 allows us to see the uphill challenge that Linda faced in convincing Mother Teresa to grant her permission to photograph her work.

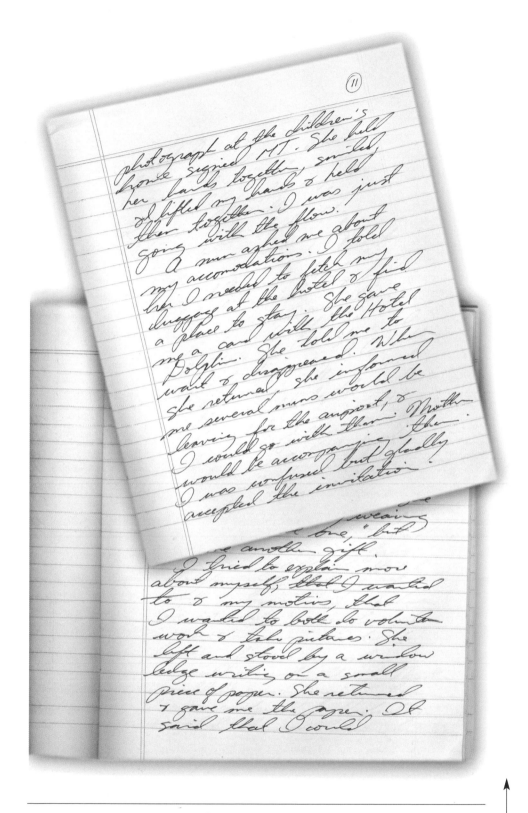

These two pages reveal the great elation felt when Mother Teresa finally gave in to Linda's pleading for an opportunity to photograph her work and permitted access to the orphans at Shishu Bhawan. The door had been opened.

Volunteer George Van den Berg, who left his job in a potato factory in Holland, poses outside the Salvation Army hostel on Sudder Street.

A quiet moment in the rain — a silhouetted volunteer holds a baby and gazes out on the courtyard of an orphanage.

M ary Hjelm, a prenatal intensive care nurse from Seattle took two months from her work to care for Mother Teresa's children in Calcutta.

V olunteer Sally Martin presents Mother Teresa with a donation at the end of her stay in Calcutta.

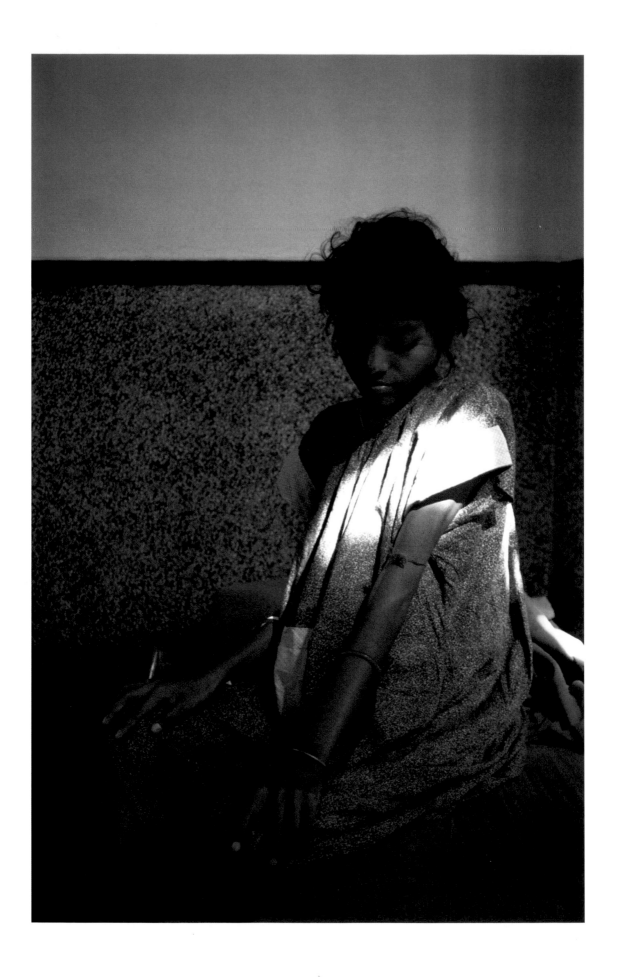

CHAPTER 8

Kalighat — Home for the Dying and Destitute

ONCE MOTHER TERESA GAVE ME PERMISSION to photograph the Mission's facilities, my enthusiasm took over — as it always does when I'm behind a camera. But after a few weeks of working in the context of both a volunteer and a photographer, I found myself exhausted. Coping with Calcutta was tiring in itself. After Mass one morning, Mother Teresa approached me and suggested that instead of taking so many pictures, that I should consider working as a volunteer at Kalighat.

Except for those very personal moments with Mother Teresa, I found that my experience in Calcutta up until that morning leaned more toward the role of an observer rather than a participant. I was accustomed to being the photographer and focusing on others doing their work. But now Mother Teresa was forcing me to put down the cameras in order to relate to her mission on a deeper level. The process of finding commitment through an open heart that began with my sick husband would be given a new meaning when I had to relate to strangers who were dying.

I looked at Mother Teresa with mixed emotions. I loved her for caring enough about me to give me this direction, but I also perceived her as a teacher who was challenging her student to go beyond her level of endurance or what she considered her limitations.

By this time, I had also changed accommodations and moved to the less expensive Circular Hotel across the street from Motherhouse. It was here that I developed a

←——————————————————

"Heaven is found by serving the lowliest."

—Mother Teresa

Mother Teresa's original mission, Nirmal Hriday — the place of the pure heart — has treated over 100,000 people since it opened its doors.

Finding peace in dying: This man appeared so close to the door of death, but sat in stillness and peace in this home filled with love and compassion.

During the time I volunteered at Kalighat I enjoyed sharing moments with this woman. She appeared far healthier than many of the men and women — however as volunteers we weren't informed of patients' conditions.

deep friendship with Esther Crowe, a long-term volunteer from Canada who had already spent months working at Kalighat.

As I began to write about this experience I received a letter from Esther with a very moving narrative based on her experiences with the Missionaries of Charity, particularly working as volunteer in Kalighat. She called Mother Teresa a "Rose of the Gutter." "For me to be identified with that Rose was beyond my comprehension. You could call her a saint. You could call her a diamond — a rough diamond it would have to be. She is so practical. She is frugal. She's got charisma. She's got zeal and she is uncompromising when it comes to helping mankind — and the gutter smell was ever so fragrant."

During the time I was in Calcutta, I heard that a wealthy businessman had offered to donate washing machines to Kalighat. Mother Teresa turned him down. She said that permitting the donation would require hiring men to maintain the equipment. Besides, laundry duty was one of the key roles for volunteers at the facility. Mother Teresa's austere life was typical of those on a serious spiritual path. She often said that the Sisters of the Missionaries of Charity lived as simple a life as those they served. Modern conveniences would only interfere with the work and her philosophy on leading a simple life.

Most of the volunteers who worked at Nirmal Hriday (place of Immaculate Heart of Mary), commonly known as Kalighat, took a public bus from Motherhouse at 7:30 each morning to reach the home for the dying and destitute by 8 o'clock.

On my first morning I recall taking a taxi because I wanted to be alone to prepare myself emotionally for this experience. I had already taken the same taxi ride on one of my early days in Calcutta when I visited the famous temple of the Goddess Kali that adjoins Mother Teresa's home for the dying. Besides the box of chocolates that I had brought for Mother Teresa from her Sisters in Atlanta, I also had gifts for Sister Delores, the Mother who was now in charge of Kalighat. She had been the Mission's Atlanta-based supervisor when an AIDS hospice was opened in there.

Kalighat is one of the busiest sections of Calcutta, with the temple drawing hundreds of worshippers daily. It was pouring rain the day a Belgian tourist, Sarah, and I were dropped off outside the ancient Hindu temple. We found cover from the rain under one of the many stalls that sell a colorful array of spiritual souvenirs, including brightly painted glazed statues of the numerous Hindu Gods. I bought a small statue of the elephant God Ganesh, known as the remover of obstacles.

Sarah and I managed to maneuver our way over puddles and through the congested traffic toward the entrance of the temple. A priest quickly offered his

Dying alone on the streets: Curled up in obvious pain, this man is left ignored and unattended by those around him. Some refuse to be taken to the home for the dying, but as Mother Teresa said, "No one is allowed to die on the streets. Someone, somewhere will bring him to us."

Mary Ellen Moore is a long-term volunteer with the Sisters. A professional nurse from New Hampshire, she assists the Sisters in administering medicines to the patients.

services as a guide for a small donation. In spite of the rain, dozens of people were crowded around their favorite deities, throwing flowers and other offerings at their painted feet.

After we completed our tour we huddled under an umbrella and drank coffee from small clay pots as we contemplated visiting Mother Teresa's home for the dying. We didn't have far to go. A large crucifix was visible on top of the dome of the temple. We climbed the worn marble stairs that thousands of the city's sick and abandoned had been carried up on stretchers by the Sisters and volunteers.

We entered a small reception area, our wet cotton pants clinging to our legs. Before anyone noticed us, I quickly surveyed our surroundings. On my left I saw the men's hall and I held my breath as I scanned the room. Emaciated bodies were huddled on blue plastic-lined cots that were numbered and placed in neat rows across the long room. Skylights dimly lighted the area, but there was a beauty in that light, a reflection of a stronger light from a divine source. Half a dozen volunteers were quietly going about their afternoon chores.

A Sister walked by with some medicines and didn't seem surprised to see these two strangers standing in the middle of the room. I asked her if the Mother in charge was available and pointed to the wet paper bag I was carrying that contained the presents from Atlanta.

Within minutes the Mother joined us and smiled, recognizing me from Atlanta. She accepted the soggy bag with childish delight. She again suggested that I might want to spend some time at Kalighat working as a volunteer. I cleared my throat, thinking at that moment that Kalighat was not one of the homes I planned to spend too much time in, but I thanked her for the offer.

Meanwhile I saw Sarah staring blankly at her surroundings. I couldn't read her emotions. Although a tourist from Belgium on this trip, Sarah often came to India on business. I met her at the Fairlawn Hotel, and she was more interested in having fun during her stay in Calcutta than visiting Mother Teresa's homes.

That night, however, Sarah had a revelation when we went to Motherhouse for the Hour of Adoration. I closed my eyes and meditated as I listened to the rhythmic sounds of the rosary being recited. When I looked up, Sarah was no longer beside me. Worried, I rushed out of the room, amazed by what I saw. Sarah was crying on a bench beside Mother Teresa. For the first time, I recognized that Sarah's defenses were shattered and her normally sophisticated, confident manner was transformed into that of a small child crying in her mother's arms. It could have been me or anyone like me who tries so hard to show the world our stronger side rather than the vulnerable one. As Mother Teresa consoled Sarah, she gave her one of those tiny medallions that were proudly worn by the volunteers, as if they were made of gold.

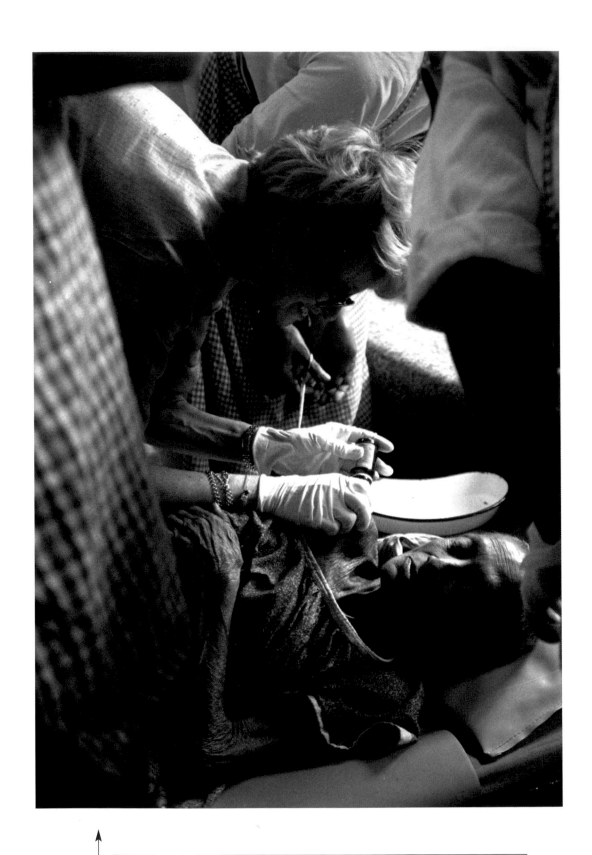

Finding joy in the work.

Later that evening while Sarah and I walked back to our hotel, she told me that as she was sitting and listening to the prayers in the presence of Mother Teresa, she was suddenly overcome by painful emotions and had left the room in tears. In an unusual move, Mother Teresa followed her outside. She told Mother Teresa how helpless she felt when she saw all of the poverty and hunger in the streets of Calcutta. "What can one person do?" she asked Mother Teresa.

In response, Mother Teresa told her that each person could make a difference when there are so many suffering people in the world. It was clear that those words touched Sarah's heart. Her eyes glistened with the joy that Mother Teresa's loving concern gives to those who unburden themselves to her.

When I climbed those worn stairs for the second time, now as a volunteer without cameras, I recalled that experience with Sarah and knew that I still carried the weight of so many sorrows, particularly the one over my first husband's death.

I joined the other volunteers in a loose circle around the Mother in charge as she began her daily message that was intended to uplift our spirits for the challenges that would face us during the day. This was a woman who had traveled to remote parts of the world for over twenty years in the service of the Missionaries of Charity, before being called home to work in Mother Teresa's favorite home. When she finished speaking, we bowed our heads in prayer. I prayed that I could open my heart to the patients in Kalighat.

I tied an apron around my waist and followed the other female volunteers over to the women. Dozens of patients waited, some lying down, others huddled over their knees in pain. One or two were limping down the aisles, using a bed or wall for support. They all required a great deal of care — they needed to be fed, bathed, soothed, and loved.

That first day as I was in training, I tried my best to be of assistance to the Sisters and other volunteers. First, the plastic-lined cots had to be washed down and the linens changed. Several women moved patients while their beds were being made with sun-dried sheets. Others were occupied preparing breakfast on aluminum plates. A hard-boiled egg and a banana accompanied generous portions of puffed rice or bread.

I helped pass out the food and cups of milky tea to the women. No sooner had I passed one row of women than I would see a woman in the back holding out her cup for more tea. Most of the women skillfully scooped the food into their mouths with their fingers, but some needed the help of a volunteer. I sat next to an elderly woman whose loose garment barely covered her skeletal frame, urging her to eat small pieces of banana that I mashed with a spoon. She looked at me

Bringing happiness to the dying — a young novice
dresses a patient in clothes made by lepers.

with sorrowful eyes, but they also reflected the love she was receiving at this home.

One couldn't help but notice that most of the women's heads were shaved. When they are rescued from the streets, many are infected with lice, so their hair is immediately shaved off as a protective measure when admitted to the hospice.

The morning passed by quickly. No sooner had the breakfast been served than it was time to clean the dishes and help the Sisters bathe the patients. I found that most of the volunteers found a favorite niche at Kalighat. While some preferred taking care of the patients, others enjoyed the vigorous laundry duty or kitchen detail. At first, I worked in the kitchen scouring the aluminum dishes with ash, but later I chose to stay with the patients and attend to their needs.

One of the most demanding jobs was bathing the women and then dressing them in fresh cotton gowns. I wasn't aware of the home's regulations — one being that two women are required to lift a patient by the shoulders and feet before carrying her over to the bathroom facilities. In spite of my own thin frame at the time, I was very strong and didn't hesitate to lift one of the women into my arms by myself. As I walked towards the Sisters with this woman who was half my size, they looked at me aghast and said, "No, no, you must have help."

I found a particular kinship with several of the patients just as I had at the orphanage. One was a woman who seemed too young to be living in a home for the dying. Since the patients' prognoses are confidential, I never knew why she had been brought to Kalighat. In spite of her deteriorating body, this woman seemed feisty and ate well. She also loved to have her body massaged with coconut oil. She would talk to me in a boisterous voice as I rubbed oil on her bald head, and although I didn't understand a word she was saying, we communicated very well.

Each day, when she saw me, this young woman would point to her body, letting me know she was ready for a massage. I enjoyed those intimate moments. We were two women, each on our own journey, but somehow united along our paths for a particular reason — both needing each other.

Esther, my friend from the Circular Hotel, was always smiling as she passed out quantities of tea. She wrote, "Then comes the time for lovin' and talking to the patients. You can speak in your own language. It doesn't have to be Bengali or Hindi. They understand perfectly. Why do you think Mother doesn't invest in washing machines, dryers, and dishwashers? Is there a miserly side to her character? Absolutely not. She is frugal, but this is not a financial matter. Mother is shrewd. She knows psychology. She knows where barriers and egos crumble, and how to integrate the most [dissimilar] group[s] from around the world in a jiffy.

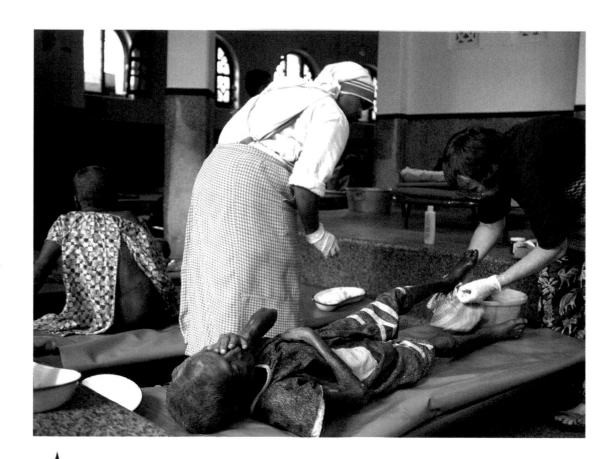

Tender care — a volunteer bathes a patient's infected foot as a Sister supervises.

O ne of the chief duties for volunteers at the home for the dying is the daily arduous task of washing patients' clothing. The young Japanese man standing on the left came down with tuberculosis from his contact with patients at the house of the dying.

100

A father and son — both with leprosy — appeared at Kalighat, the Calcutta house of the dying, before finding a home at Titagarh, the leper colony.

Moreover, the adrenaline kicks in. You are on a spiritual high. The ripple effect is infinite."

A much needed mid-morning break gave the volunteers a chance to lounge on the roof of the building and drink tea with some hard biscuits and jelly. We talked and laughed about everything from what brought us here, to how we were planning to continue our lives once we left Mother Teresa's world.

We were of all ages and came from all parts of the world. Each day I saw George from Holland, hard at work, dumping armfuls of dirty laundry into a huge, round metal pot where he and several other men would spend hours scrubbing out the dirt. Then they would carry the nearly clean laundry up to the oddly shaped roof where they helped an Indian woman lay out the clothes to dry on the hot tile.

I joined them several times and enjoyed those hours in the scorching sun trying to find a space between sheets to add another wet one. It also provided a wonderful bird's-eye view over the bustling streets of Kalighat. It was an amazing environment: here we were, on top of a Hindu temple with a statue of Jesus facing this building — a building that was devoted to a Goddess known for her ruthlessness in cutting out evil from the hearts of man.

Later, when I returned to the Circular Hotel before lunch, I would soak my feet in a bucket of hot water and scrub my hands and legs with Detinol, an anti-bacterial soap. I never used the plastic gloves that were available to the volunteers or a mask over my face. Unfortunately, one young man from the Orient did develop tuberculosis after being exposed to it at Kalighat, but I never saw him leave the city. I did notice, however, that Mother Teresa paid special attention to him.

Some evenings Esther and I would roam the city looking for a new place to eat, but most of the time we had dinner at our hotel. A retired plumber from New York City often joined us along with other volunteers. His vitality and dedication to Mother Teresa amazed me. He was basically living fulltime at the Circular Hotel and using his own money to paint the metal bed frames at Kalighat and to patch up leaking pipes.

I finally felt like part of the gang, a member of the corps of volunteers. We were easily identifiable in Calcutta. Anyone dressed in old cotton clothes, shoes, and socks and walking through the streets of Calcutta had to be working for Mother Teresa. The businessmen and tourists generally stayed within the walls of the more fashionable hotels.

On one of my last days at Kalighat a young boy came crying into the facility with his sick mother. She was given a cot to lie down on until the Sisters could attend to her. I was told that the woman had stomach cancer, and as she groaned

Mother Teresa often quoted the Prayer of St. Francis: "Lord, make me a channel of thy peace, . . . that where there is despair, I may bring hope; that where there are shadows, I may bring light."

on the bed holding her arms around her waist, I sat beside her and began lightly massaging her body. The groans ceased as she drifted off to sleep.

This was my most heartfelt experience at Kalighat. I felt this woman's pain, as if it had been my late husband's cancer. But now I could reach towards her without the terror. I felt only great compassion toward this dying woman who would leave a small child behind. Mother Teresa helped me heal my own wounds as I helped this woman. She gives all of us the opportunity to transcend our own pain by working through it with love.

It was also a relief to leave the cameras at the hotel. I only photographed at Kalighat after I had been working there as a volunteer and when the patients and Sisters were familiar with my presence. It was beautiful to see something different through the lens. They were not the subjects of a spectator or journalist, but people with whom I had shared an important part of my life. I know that many of the women I met have left their bodies behind by now, but their souls have been given a lasting tribute by Mother Teresa.

A few weeks after I had been at Kalighat, the Mother in charge told me that I looked tired and should take a break. A few days later I decided to visit Varanasi, one of India's most holy cities, located on the banks of the Ganges River. I would find Mother Teresa's presence there as well, in a home for the dying, once a palace supposedly owned by a King of Nepal.

104

The city of Varanasi on the River Ganges is one of the oldest cities in the world. It is the place where Buddha preached his first sermon and where most of the world's religions are represented. Alongside the famous temples and palaces is a home for the dying operated by the Missionaries of Charity and supposedly once owned by a King of Nepal.

CHAPTER 9

Varanasi: City of Pilgrims — and Mother Teresa's Home for the Dying

* * * *

IN PREPARATION FOR MY OVERNIGHT TRAIN RIDE to Varanasi, I bought chains and locks to strap my camera equipment to my bunk. After I had crossed the river on a ferry to the Howrah railroad station and entered the frenetic chaos of one of India's busiest stations, I was suddenly overcome with terror at the prospect of taking this second journey alone.

I managed to locate my train and climbed the dusty, iron stairs of the second class, air-conditioned compartment. I was fortunate to obtain a ticket on short notice due to a tourist quota that restricts the number of seats for foreigners. Reservations must be made well in advance. India's railroad transportation system, developed under the British rule, is still the main form of travel in the country. Although the airline industry has expanded over the last few years, it is still far too expensive for most people.

When I found my bottom bunk, an Indian couple who shared the same cubicle were already preparing their home-cooked food out of metal containers. Later they told me that they were making their yearly pilgrimage to their Guru's ashram in a city a few stops past Varanasi. As I secured my camera bags, it suddenly occurred to me that I had completely forgotten about bringing food and only had a bottle of water to sustain me. After the train left the station a vendor came by with a tray filled with hot, spicy meals in cardboard boxes. I knew better than to put my fragile stomach through that challenge.

I had been told at the tourist office that this was an express train and that we would arrive in Varanasi by the following morning. Instead, I was shocked to discover that it was a mail train and that we would stop at every station along the route. For the next twenty hours I tried to fill my empty stomach with crackers and water which I had brought with me. Fortunately I caught up on much needed sleep and between naps ventured out onto the railroad platforms to videotape some very colorful scenes.

People from all over the world have traveled to Varanasi for over two thousand years. Worshipers come to the famous bathing *ghats* at dawn each morning to glorify Lord Siva the famous Hindu God who is said to have made Varanasi his home.

I was amazed that even in remote, rural parts of India, public areas are usually still bustling with activity. When we pulled into a station, vendors selling everything from fruit to fried foods and soft drinks quickly appeared trying to attract us with their goods. At one stop I saw families cuddled together, sleeping on the bare ground. The cries of a baby woke his mother. She quickly uncovered a fold in her sari as she pulled the hungry child to her breast. I videotaped beggars holding out their hands for a few rupees and when they saw me, they wailed out, "Mama, mama." In the midst of this activity, a cow searched for morsels of leftover food between the sleeping bodies.

When we finally reached Varanasi, I opened the shade on my window and had my first breathtaking view of the city. Ancient buildings hovered over the banks of the Ganges in a scene reminiscent of an impressionist painting. The pastel colors blended into a spectacular design of shadow and light.

This holy city has changed hands numerous times over thousands of years, and each conquering nation has left its mark behind. Even after countless attempts by invaders to destroy religious landmarks, new temples replaced the old ones, and vestiges of the city's history are still apparent today. I could see the top of a Muslim temple next to a Hindu shrine. Each religion seems to be represented in this spiritual haven. As the sun set, the palatial buildings reflected in the water seemed to hang like ornaments over the peaceful river.

No sooner had I stepped off the train, than the usual tenacious group of taxi drivers tried to befriend me with promises of taking me to the best accommodations at reasonable rates. I chose to go with a driver who spoke adequate English and seemed at home with foreign tourists.

He drove me to a modest, but clean hotel not far from the center of town. After I had changed out of my traveling clothes and drank two cups of strong Indian coffee, my guide offered to take me to a factory where I could videotape men weaving silk saris and scarves. It was already dark by now, but a group of men remained hunched over their looms, swiftly weaving intricate designs using gold, luminescent green, and pink threads. I was reminded of Mother Teresa's lepers who were equally skillful at their looms, but the women who were accustomed to the luxury of silk would never wear the cotton saris they created.

I was amazed by the stamina of the men. In this factory I learned that apprenticeship into the trade began when boys were barely eight years of age, and if they survived the hardships over the years, they became master weavers by fifteen. Their wages were low and so was their working life span, since eventually their eyesight deteriorated from the arduous work.

I was fortunate to have arrived in Varanasi for the Duvali festival of lights that honors the Divine Mother. It is the time of year to clean out the old in order

A grandmother surrounded by "tent children" in the slums that are part of life in India.

M oment of worship: An expectant woman is silhouetted against the rays of the early morning sun in Varanasi. The Hindus call this city "Kashi" — the Luminous, the City of Light.

to bring in the new. Offerings are made to Laxmi, Goddess of Wealth, for a prosperous New Year. As we drove through the alleys of the city, I saw dozens of *pujas*, or prayer altars, sparkling with candlelight, as priests recited the time-consuming Vedic prayers that date back thousands of years.

Varanasi, also known as Banaras, is most famous for its bathing *ghats* [steps]. It is considered by Indians to be one of their holiest cities — a major pilgrimage center for people throughout the country and the world. The mazes of narrow, cobble-stoned streets leading to the *ghats* are always bursting with excited pilgrims as they head for the numerous temples for their spiritual renewal.

Many elderly Indians come to this city for their final resting place, because it is believed that bathing in the Ganges at this site assures liberation for the soul. It is the home of Siva, the main Hindu God who symbolizes both the creator and destroyer.

Early the next morning I quickly dressed and raced down to the *ghats* in a motorized rickshaw. I found the sleepy owner of a rowboat and agreed to a price for a tour down the river so that I could photograph the first bathers as the sun rose. We floated past each uniquely built palace, and with a 200mm lens, I began framing my shots. Women in saris and men dressed in ceremonial white dhotis climbed off the steps and slipped into the sacred water. Some of the men wore a thread across their chests, which indicates that they were born into the highest class of Brahmins, which includes priests and educators.

I photographed a sea of hands lifted in prayer, as water spilled back into the river from their palms. We passed the crematorium *ghat* where I captured several scenes of bodies wrapped in gold paper lying on wooden stretchers, being prepared for their departure from earth.

I thought that I was leaving Calcutta and the Missionaries of Charity behind for a while, but as we rowed past a large white stucco building, I was told that it was a home for the dying, opened by Mother Teresa.

That afternoon I went by foot through the maze of streets in search of the home, but got completely lost. Then suddenly, from around a corner, appeared two Sisters dressed in the blue and white saris of the Missionaries of Charity. I couldn't believe my good fortune.

I approached the women and told them briefly about my experience as a volunteer in Calcutta. We hailed a rickshaw and within minutes were outside of the home. They invited me into a quiet, open courtyard where I found myself in yet another sanctuary so similar to the other homes run by the Missionaries of Charity.

Mother Teresa said that the last moments of a person's life are some of the most important — and they should not be alone at that time.

According to Hindu tradition, a person who dies in Varanasi is guaranteed *moksha* or liberation from the cycle of life and death. Mother Teresa's Indian Sisters are very familiar with the various religions of their homeland, and give their patients the burial of their faith.

L ooking into the eyes of compassion at the home of the dying.

Sr. Alphonsa of Kerala (India) is in charge of the home for the dying in Varanasi. She was a large, stately, imposing woman with a warm heart. We looked over the magnificent banks of the Ganges and talked well into the evening.

A colorful view of the Dasashvamedh *ghat* — the *ghat* of the ten (*Das*) horses (*shiva*) sacrificed (*medh*) — from a rented boat on the Ganges reveals pilgrims who come for a ritual bath and to perform *puja* to the rising sun, following a centuries-old tradition.

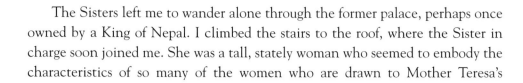

The Sisters left me to wander alone through the former palace, perhaps once owned by a King of Nepal. I climbed the stairs to the roof, where the Sister in charge soon joined me. She was a tall, stately woman who seemed to embody the characteristics of so many of the women who are drawn to Mother Teresa's organization.

As we watched the sun setting over the Ganges we discussed the differences between Hinduism and Christianity. In a city where death is accepted as part of the cycle of rebirth, the Sisters are more concerned with the immediate needs of serving the dying. I found that the Mother in charge was not judgmental of Hindi belief systems, but was providing a Christian-based service to those of any faith who needed shelter and loving hands to help them through their last days.

I enjoyed this peaceful moment and the openness between two women of opposite backgrounds sharing their perspectives on a normally controversial subject. By now I had found that the Sisters were more than willing to take the time to discuss issues or concerns related to their Order or to life in general. She excused herself to take care of some errands and gave me permission to photograph in the patients' quarters.

The men's rooms were not as active as Kalighat, but there was that familiar, serene atmosphere. I sat and talked with a few of the men who understood English. They seemed to enjoy my company although they weren't accustomed to foreign visitors. They gracefully allowed me to photograph them, and as I became involved in my work, I almost forgot that I was scheduled to leave Varanasi by train that evening.

The Sisters immediately offered to drive me to the station. Cramped in a tiny car, we chatted like old friends during the hour-long drive. It was even suggested that I might find happiness as one of them — a Sister of the Missionaries of Charity. I laughed and told her that I was too much of a free spirit, but that I would always be motivated by my work to search for those who had given their lives in the service of God.

The Sisters waited on the platform with me for the train to arrive and then helped carry my luggage on board. This was an express train, and we did arrive in Calcutta the next morning. My encounter with the Sisters of Varanasi was further confirmation for me that this journey was being guided by a higher power.

Quiet moments at the home for the dying in Varanasi. When I first entered the lavish structure of the home, I was offered a cup of Indian tea. It was wonderful to be in the cool surroundings of the courtyard and off the noisy and crowded streets of Varanasi.

Situated on the crescent-shaped left bank of the holy Ganges, Varanasi, one of the ancient seats of learning in India, is said to be a compound of the names of two streams, the Varuna and the Assi, which still flow in the north and south of the city respectively. It is considered a privilege to die in Varanasi. These bodies will be cremated on the banks of the Ganges. Any pilgrimage to "Kashi" includes rites for the dead and ashes are often brought to be spread along the river.

Final vows handwritten by each of the novices — many stay up all night to prepare them — held tightly in the hand of Mother Teresa.

CHAPTER 10

Final Vows — Special Mass

❋ ❋ ❋ ❋

A FEW DAYS AFTER RETURNING TO CALCUTTA from Varanasi, Sister Deena who oversaw the volunteers asked me if I would be interested in photographing two very special ceremonies for the Motherhouse at the end of November. One was a Mass during which the novices would be taking their first vows and the other was a Mass for the Sisters taking their final vows as lifelong members of the Missionaries of Charity.

I was stunned by this request since, as a rule, Mother Teresa and her organization rarely requested such services from a photographer. But now I was being given the opportunity to document the most sacred events of the year held by the Missionaries of Charity. I would be working for the woman I most admired in the world! I told Sister Deena that I would be leaving for a brief trip to Bangalore, but would return to Calcutta in time for both masses.

Two weeks later, I registered for a second time at the Circular Hotel. In preparation for my assignment I had purchased film in Bangalore, but the battery pack for my flash unit was out of power. The recharger had blown up — overheated by the Indian electricity system. As a photographer, I was in a terrible dilemma. I didn't have the technical equipment necessary for my assignment.

As a last resort, I tracked down a camera repair shop in an alley behind a clothing merchandise warehouse. The man who owned the shop couldn't help me but was very considerate, sending one of his employees to accompany me to scout for electrical stores that might carry a compatible unit for my flash. We walked through the maze of streets near Howrah Station and into half a dozen shops without success.

I prayed on a street corner for a few seconds, and then my companion and I crossed the street to the last shop in the area. The tall man behind the counter took one look at my battery and without a word, turned and found a contraption on the shelf. He cut a few wires and plugged it into my unit. I was astonished to see a green light suddenly turn on. It actually worked!

With Mother Teresa walking nearby, novices, some of whom have been in training for up to seven years, hold their personal vows to the order as they walk to the Mass that will culminate in them becoming Sisters of the Missionaries of Charity.

Novices continue to grow in number, despite faltering attendance in other orders. Here a group gathers to watch the ceremony from a balcony.

The final steps toward making a life-long commitment to the order. Mother Teresa made her final vows on May 24, 1937 in Darjeeling, India.

Families, friends, and volunteers join the Sisters in the "profession of vows" ceremonies at St. Mary's Church.

The Missionaries of Charity is an international order. A young Belgian woman receives the Eucharist from an Indian priest after taking her final vows.

The training is intense, the commitment lifelong. It was clear these Sisters had made that decision.

Mother Teresa watched over her Sisters with the tender look of a true mother as they took their vows.

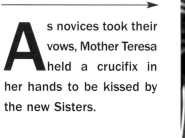

As novices took their vows, Mother Teresa held a crucifix in her hands to be kissed by the new Sisters.

During the two days of "The Ceremony of Religious Profession of Vows" at St. Mary's Mother Teresa appeared very serious and anxious — as would any parent. Immediately afterward I was amazed by the transformation in her demeanor. All the volunteers, family members, and Sisters were invited to the Motherhouse for a celebration. We gathered on the rooftop, and for the first time Mother Teresa posed for my camera in an animated fashion — as if the entire process I had gone through with her was a divine joke. She smiled for my camera as she gathered the Sisters around her. The joy she found through her work was so clear, particularly through the love she gave her Sisters. It was truly a great honor to be included in such an important moment of Mother Teresa's life.

I dashed out of the store and jumped into a taxi. I needed two hours to recharge my battery, and would have only minutes to spare to get to St. Mary's near Motherhouse on time for the Mass.

This had to be the most excruciating experience I had ever had in my career. Mother Teresa was opening yet another door to me, and I had come very close to not making it through. "Another one of God's tests," I thought as I rushed to the church. I was as ready as I had ever been for a photographic assignment.

The novices taking their first vows had already formed a line outside the sanctuary. Mother Teresa was hovering over her latest group of soon-to-be Sisters. It was clear to me at that moment that these smiling women were not only entering the service of God, but that they were completely committed to the tiny woman whom they called "Mother."

The Sister in charge of the Mass approached me and gave me a general overview of what to expect during the ceremony. I joined several local news photographers near the altar and found a corner on the floor in front of a Sister where I could sit cross-legged. At that moment I felt as if I was about to photograph the most important event of my life. My hands trembled as I loaded my cameras with film. I surveyed my surroundings and scouted the scenes through my lens in preparation for the moments that I would capture on film.

The church was filled to capacity. I could see all of the volunteers in the balcony near the Missionaries of Charity choir group. The sea of faces that waited in great anticipation for the Mass to begin seemed so ordinary. Yet the women's colorful saris were so startling in contrast to the more somber attire worn in the West.

Hundreds of relatives had come from many parts of the world to witness this great event involving daughters, sisters, and nieces (see photo next page). Most of the families came from less privileged homes, while some appeared to be quite wealthy. The Missionaries of Charity attracts women from a wide spectrum of race, religion, and economic backgrounds.

Then the choir leader raised her hand, and as the devotional singing began, Mother Teresa gracefully accompanied her novices down the aisle to a pew in front of the altar. An Indian priest gave a homily based on the theme of service and sacrifice — a life that the novices were about to enter as Sisters of the Missionaries of Charity.

Mother Teresa approached the altar and waited to receive each novice's handwritten vow. She looked tenderly at the women as she held a crucifix up to their faces. After Mother Teresa accepted the vows, the young women had to bend over in order to kiss the cross of Jesus that Mother Teresa held in her hand. Many tears flowed during the conclusion of the ceremony.

Following the Mass I photographed many of the joyful Sisters with their equally happy families. Later that day I developed the film, prepared a book of photographs, and presented it to Mother Teresa and the Order. Sister Deena told me that the book itself was a luxury that they couldn't accept nor did they have a place to store it. However, she said the Sisters would be grateful for the photographs.

Two days later when I photographed the Sisters making their final vows at St. Mary's, I felt Mother Teresa's presence in a way that I had never experienced. The church vibrated with the devotion and love of the Divine Mother. The female presence was so strong, so tender, and yet so powerful.

As I photographed the Sisters presenting their hand-written vows to Mother Teresa, *bhakti* (devotional) tears flowed down my face. This is what I had truly always wanted to experience. I was finally working in the service of this saintly woman whose humble presence embraced us all. As the Sisters took their vows, I felt we were all sharing in the process of making a deeper commitment to God. The experience in St. Mary's that day was like floating in the womb of the Divine Mother.

East and West meet in Calcutta: After the "Profession of Vows" ceremonies I photographed many of the families with their daughters — now Missionaries of Charity. Pride was so evident on the faces — although expressed differently — of those who had come to witness this historic event. Some families had traveled hundreds of miles from rural India, while others had flown to Calcutta from Europe. The pride in their children was equal.

After the ceremony we were all invited to Motherhouse for a celebration. The normally peaceful courtyard was buzzing with activity and laughter. And then, Mother Teresa appeared, surrounded by her Sisters, with garlands of flowers around their necks.

I squeezed my way through the crowd as if my life depended on it. I knew that I was about to get the photograph of a lifetime. For the first time, Mother Teresa posed in front of my camera with her Sisters, and they laughed with such joy. As I clicked the shutter, my heart pounding, Mother Teresa looked at me as if to say, "Are you finally happy?" "Yes, yes," I answered from my heart.

Honoring Mary: Following the ceremony of Religious Profession of Vows, the Sisters adorned the statue of Mary in the prayer room at the Motherhouse with one of their own saris.

Lady of Love

God sent an angel to some of the poorest streets of the world.

Lady of Love

So pure of spirit

Clothed in the robes of God

Lady of love, you are in my heart

I heard your call: "come and see"

Looking into your eyes, I saw how God worked through you

I touched your feet, and you touched me

You were the greatest mother of all

Lady of love, I miss you

— **Linda Schaefer**

In a view rarely seen, Mother Teresa showed her humorous side when she gave her Sisters a thumbs up for job well done.

CHAPTER 11

Final Blessing

❄ ❄ ❄ ❄

AFTER THE FINAL VOWS CEREMONIES, I flew to a spiritual community in South India to meet my new husband for Christmas. One month later he flew back to Atlanta, and I decided to make a last journey to Calcutta for what would become Mother Teresa's final blessing.

I was very nauseous when I boarded the plane for this third trip to Calcutta. Within a few days I discovered that I was pregnant. When I received the joyous news in a small medical clinic, I knew that God had intervened. "Finally," I thought, "I'm going to have a baby."

I quickly made preparations to return to the United States. The night before my departure, I took my last rickshaw ride to Motherhouse for the Hour of Adoration. I prayed that I would be able to personally say good-bye to Mother Teresa.

She was seated in her usual position on her mat near the door. I looked at her and silently asked her not to disappear after the rosary. However, before the hour was over, Mother Teresa got up and walked out the door. I looked at the statue of the Virgin Mary and thanked her for this memorable time in my life.

When I walked out into the corridor, Mother Teresa was leaning on the verandah wall. I was so relieved to see her and immediately walked up to her. She looked at me with a knowing glance and placed her hand over my head. I felt the radiance of her touch traveling to my womb. I told her that I was going home. "Oh, to New York?" she asked me. "No, to Atlanta," I responded. "Please give my Sisters there my love." Those were her final words to me. She seemed so frail, yet so strong as I gazed one last time into those eyes that reflected wisdom and kindness

❄ ❄ ❄ ❄

When asked who would take her place at the Missionaries of Charity, Mother Theresa said: "The world will understand that it is not my work. It is God's. It will go on."

Two years later, I held my young son and cried at my pain and loss when I heard the news of Mother Teresa's death. "She has merged with the eternal flame of divinity," I thought with deep sadness. But I knew that she would always be a flame in my heart.

One night in a dream, I saw Mother Teresa holding and rocking my son. When I awoke, I knew that Mother Teresa's final blessing was also shared with the child that I brought into the world.

❊   ❊   ❊   ❊

" **I** must not attempt to control God's actions. I must not count the stages in the journey he would have me make. I must not desire a clear perception of my advance along the road. Nor know precisely where I am on the way to holiness. I ask him to make a saint of me, yet I must leave to him the choice of the means which lead to it."

— **Mother Teresa**

CHAPTER 12

Woman of the Century

❊   ❊   ❊   ❊

MOTHER TERESA'S STRONG DESIRE TO BECOME A NUN in the slums of Calcutta was eventually answered. However, there was a long waiting period. She had taken the route required. She joined the Loretto Order and spent her time in Ireland before being sent to India. But there was always an irresistible urge to go outside of the safe walls of the convent and to work directly with the poorest of the poor. These desires drove her, and as a result, she became one of the greatest influences on humanity in our time.

I roamed the streets of Calcutta for months. I walked on the railroad tracks where so many of the poor lived in cardboard boxes. But I could never hope to see these people through Mother Teresa's eyes.

The British had left Calcutta behind and Mother Teresa rediscovered it. The city was graced by having a living saint in their midst. She went to the people in the slums and gave them her heart. "Come and see," she said. I could only see a glimpse of what she saw through those beautiful eyes, but I feel so fortunate to have been in her presence and to have looked into the soul of compassion.

I first met her two years before she died. It was near the end of the twentieth century. She was a woman who wore a cross near her heart. She never publicized her work, but she was awarded the Nobel Peace Prize.

If there is a prize awarded for the Woman of the Century, I believe it would go to Mother Teresa. She embodied the message that we hope will grow more prevalent in the new century — the message of love.

❊   ❊   ❊   ❊

Greetings at St. Mary's, Calcutta: Mother Teresa allowed her hand to be held by all who came to her. Before a Mass, she greeted an army officer in the same manner she greeted a priest.

* * * *

Under the watchful eyes of cameras, Mother Teresa humbly turns over the vows of her Sisters and partic-pates in Holy Communion.

Epilogue – 2003

✳ ✳ ✳ ✳

IN THE YEARS SINCE MOTHER TERESA'S DEATH, the documentary work I produced in Calcutta, has taken me on a number of paths. The commitment that I made to her in 1995 marked my unwavering faith in her work and my tiny participation in the legacy she would leave to the world. Together with experts in the field, I have refined my experience into a book along with other printed materials. That, together with numerous speaking engagements, has given me a sense of security that Mother Teresa is always present in my life.

In August 1997, I brought my nine-month-old son Paul to India, hoping that he would have the opportunity to meet Mother Teresa. My son and I were visiting the *ashram* (spiritual community) of another beloved Indian holy woman in South India when I heard the news that hot early August morning. Then I saw the headlines in the local Indian newspaper. Mother Teresa, living saint for millions and revered by the people of her adoptive country, was gone.

That day, the world mourned the passing of Mother Teresa, whose greatest mission was to help the poorest of the poor — to give them love. I recall that morning so vividly. I was seated under the canopy of dried banana leaves in the common eating area of the *ashram*, drinking milky Indian coffee, and breathing in the humid air. Tears rolled down my cheeks as I watched my son crawling around the tables (he began walking and running a month later) bringing smiles to people's faces.

It was in this same *ashram* that I read of the tragic death of Princess Diana. The lined face of Mother Teresa was such a contrast to the beautiful but sad face of the celebrity princess. There are those who thought that the worldwide attention given the princess's death took away from the passing of the holy woman. In my heart, I believe that Mother Teresa would have preferred having the attention diverted.

People have often asked me if I had a spiritual transformation as a result of being with Mother Teresa. Catholics want to know if I converted to Catholicism. My response is that Mother Teresa never asked me to convert to her faith, or even questioned me about my affiliation. Perhaps if she had advised me to convert, I might seriously have considered doing so.

The spiritual path is possibly the most challenging one a person can face in a lifetime. My first monumental step was facing the death of my first husband at a young age. My second was facing life as a single mother, following a divorce from my second husband. I have found greater equanimity in my life when I serve God through my role as a journalist who is also willing to participate in His work. It's hard to forget that Mother Teresa once held my hands firmly in her own — in a state of prayer. The empowering moments with her have helped me through many difficult times. "Pray, my child, pray," she said to me. It is comforting to know that the words she said are so true.

I'll know that I've arrived at a place of greater self-awareness, when the bothersome things of life are no longer bothersome, when the nasty tone of a voice no longer weakens me, and when I live fully in the present without any fear of the future. Until then, I walk the earth with my son, and pray for greater compassion and love for all beings.

✳ ✳ ✳ ✳